The Culturewise Guide to European Business

John Cutler

CULTUREWISE PUBLISHING
4th Floor, 16-18 Marshalsea Road, London, SE1 1HL, UK

THE CULTUREWISE GUIDE TO
EUROPEAN BUSINESS CULTURES
Copyright © John Cutler 2008

All Rights Reserved

No part of this book may be reproduced in any form, by photocopying or by any electronic or mechanical means, including information storage or retrieval systems, without permission in writing from both the copyright owner and the publisher of this book.

ISBN 978-0-9559484-0-4

First Published 2008 by
Culturewise Publishing

Printed in Great Britain for Culturewise Publishing

THE CULTUREWISE GUIDE TO EUROPEAN BUSINESS CULTURES

John Cutler

Also by John Cutler

- The Cross-cultural Communication Trainer's Manual - Volume 1.
  ISBN: 978-0-566-08701-1

- The Cross-cultural Communication Trainer's Manual - Volume 2.
  ISBN: 978-0-566-08702-8

After reading volume one - The Design of Cross-Cultural Training, and then following up with volume two - Activities for Cross-Cultural Training, it's plain that this composite work is not only highly useful but essential, as the whole field of training across cultures is dealt with in a very positive and specific manner. Both the design aspects and learning activities are extremely practical.

Useful? ★★★★★ Well-written? ★★★★★ Practical? ★★★★★ Inspirational? ★★★★★ Value for money? ★★★★★ Overall ★★★★★.

Personnel Today, January 2006

This logical progression should help any trainer who is new to the subject to design a learning programme...provides an excellent resource to develop most types of cross-cultural communication training and can be used as a solid foundation around which more specialist courses can be designed.

People Management, November 2005

Contents

Acknowledgements ix

Introduction xi

1. Italy 1
   Introduction 1
   The cultural background to business in Italy 1
     La Famiglia 1
     'Good' people 3
   Building relationships 4
   Making the right impression 5
   Persuading and influencing 6
   Dealing with hierarchies 7
   Managing people 7
   Managing time, schedules, deadlines and bureaucracy 8

2. Belgium 11
   Introduction 11
   The cultural background to business in Belgium 11
     The weight of history 11
     Authority and compromise 13
     Modesty 14
     The good life 14
   Building relationships 15
   Making the right impression 16
   Persuading and influencing 17
   Dealing with hierarchies 17
   Managing people 17
   Managing time, schedules, deadlines and bureaucracy 18

3. France 19
   Introduction 19
   The cultural background to business in France 19
     The State 19
     Rebellion, opposition and individualism 20
     The importance of hierarchy 21
     Elitism and egalitarianism 22
     French logic 23
   Building relationships 25

Making the right impression	26
Persuading and influencing	27
Dealing with hierarchies	28
Managing people	28
Managing time, schedules, deadlines and bureaucracy	29

4. Russia ... 31

Introduction	31
The cultural background to business in Russia	31
Stereotypes	31
Russian generations	33
Building relationships	34
Making the right impression	36
Persuading and influencing	37
Dealing with hierarchies	38
Managing people	39
Managing time, schedules, deadlines and bureaucracy	40

5. United Kingdom ... 43

Introduction	43
The cultural background to business in the UK	43
The British identity	43
Britain and class	44
The 'cold' British	45
The British and authority	46
British individualism	47
The education system	48
Building relationships	48
Making the right impression	50
Persuading and influencing	51
Dealing with hierarchies	52
Managing people	53
Managing time, schedules, deadlines and bureaucracy	53

6. Spain ... 55

Introduction	55
The cultural background to business in Spain	55
Individualism and connections	56
Creativity and improvisation	58
Building relationships	58
Making the right impression	59

	Persuading and influencing	60
	Dealing with hierarchies	61
	Managing people	62
	Managing time, schedules, deadlines and bureaucracy	63

7. Switzerland 65

Introduction 65
The cultural background to business in Switzerland 65
   Order, formality and consensus 65
   Neutrality, privacy, pragmatism and hard work 67
Building relationships 68
Making the right impression 69
Persuading and influencing 70
Dealing with hierarchies 71
Managing people 71
Managing time, schedules, deadlines and bureaucracy 72

8. Germany 73

Introduction 73
The cultural background to business in Germany 73
   The social market 73
   The search for truth 74
Building relationships 75
Making the right impression 75
Persuading and influencing 76
Dealing with hierarchies 78
Managing people 78
Managing time, schedules, deadlines and bureaucracy 80

9. Scandinavia 81

Introduction 81
The cultural background to business in Scandinavia 81
   The Viking heritage 81
   Lutheranism 82
   Informality 83
Building relationships 84
Making the right impression 84
Persuading and influencing 86
Dealing with hierarchies 87
Managing people 88
Managing time, schedules, deadlines and bureaucracy 88

10. The Netherlands 89

Introduction 89
The cultural background to business in The Netherlands 89
   Tolerance, consensus and compromise 89
   Calvinism and conformity 90
   Overleg and Beleid 91
Building relationships 91
Making the right impression 92
Persuading and influencing 94
Dealing with hierarchies 95
Managing people 95
Managing time, schedules, deadlines and bureaucracy 96

11. Poland 99

Introduction 99
The cultural background to business in Poland 99
   History and identity 99
   Hierarchy and conflict 100
   Religion and family 101
Building relationships 101
Making the right impression 102
Persuading and influencing 103
Dealing with hierarchies 104
Managing people 105
Managing times, schedules, deadlines and bureaucracy 106

12. Hungary 107

Introduction 107
The cultural background to business in Hungary 107
   Language and communication styles 107
   Family 108
   Hungarian 'pessimism' 109
Building relationships 110
Making the right impression 110
Persuading and influencing 112
Dealing with hierarchies 113
Managing people 113
Managing time, schedules, deadlines and bureaucracy 114

Acknowledgements

I would like to thank the excellent team of freelance cultural trainers and country experts who have assisted with many of the ideas found in these chapters. In no particular order these include Christophe Laurens, Robert Johnson, Alessandra Gnudi, Hans Buschmann, Katalina Szom-Bath, Sharjeel Moutier, Tatiana Prokyeva, Anna Chodynicka and many others. I would also like to thanks the many Culturewise clients from whom I have learnt so much.

Introduction

Cultural differences do not, in themselves, make life difficult for people living and working across cultural and linguistic boundaries. On the contrary, developing an understanding of different assumptions, expectations and ways of doing things can be an extremely enriching personal and professional experience. However cultural differences can cause difficulty in business if those of us who work across borders and cultures fail to acknowledge that other people often (although not always) think and work in different ways, or if we interpret other people's behaviour based on out-of-date and restrictive stereotypes. The purpose of *The Culturewise Guide to European Business Cultures* is to provide an introduction to some of the cultural differences that impact on the way business is conducted and people managed in 12 European countries. It aims to move beyond stereotypes to provide a source of useful, relevant and up-to-date information and advice for those new to working in Europe, or those who need to know more about a particular country or countries.

To get the best out of the *Guide* I would ask readers to bear in mind some of the following cautionary points. Firstly, the *Guide* is not and does not seek to be definitive, either in terms of the countries it covers or the information it gives about each country. It aims to provide a current snapshot of how business is done in some of the most important countries in Europe, nothing more. Cultures change and develop and the current economic crisis is likely to spur further dramatic changes across European business. Readers should always supplement their reading of the *Guide* with an understanding of issues their particular companies, markets, sectors and professions face.

Secondly, bearing in mind globalisation and the multicultural and multinational nature of many European countries and businesses, the question arises as to whether it is right for a *Guide* to focus on differences in the way business is conducted across Europe. Many people I come into contact with argue that globalisation has led to a shared European or even global 'business culture' that everyone in the world of commerce participates in, regardless of their location, ethnicity and background. I disagree. For my part I certainly recognise that there is much that all European or even global cultures and business cultures have in common. These commonalities are a good starting point in building relationships with clients, colleagues and suppliers from other cultures and traditions.

However, global convergence masks local divergence. Diversity in beliefs, attitudes and actions is one of the glories of humanity and needs to be jealously guarded. Even if some business practices are the same the world over, I still believe it is possible to identify a range of beliefs, values and behaviours that the majority of business people who live in the UK, France or Germany would recognise as being traditionally British, French or German. I do not suggest that every UK, French, German resident necessarily shares the same cultural characteristics. Europeans are as individual and unique as residents of any other part of the world. But I do believe that is possible to identify some useful, positive and helpful generalisations about cultural differences in business. The most important of these differences relate to attitudes towards status and hierarchy in the workplace; how and where business relationships are built; attitudes towards decision-making, consensus and conflict-resolution; communication styles; and the necessity for firm and fixed structures and policies in the business environment. There are other differences of course, but these are the ones that in my experience are most important for conducting cross-border business in Europe. These generalisations may help to paint a picture of some of the influences on the people with whom you come into contact across Europe, although they will certainly not hold true for every person you meet. The focus always has to be on understanding the individuals we encounter within their cultural context, but not stereotyping these individuals by assuming they necessarily fit within one or other particular cultural pattern. Cultural differences represent an opportunity for personal learning and development rather than a barrier to success or an excuse for stereotyping.

Thirdly, this guide is written from an Anglo-Saxon perspective and is deliberately designed to highlight issues that Anglo-Saxons face in working across Europe. Readers from other cultural backgrounds might benefit from a different emphasis in the various chapters, although I think there is much in the guide that anyone can learn from, regardless of their background. If your own country is featured in the *Guide* then read about it. Understanding how our own culture is perceived by others can be as educational as reading about someone else's.

Finally, the *Guide* makes suggestions about behaviours that may help you get things done more successfully in a different culture. It does not and should not demand that you change everything you do. Your first priority is to remain true to your own core values and beliefs, and to understand the behaviours that for you are, and are not, open to change. This will be different for each individual. You may choose to change, or you may choose not to change in response to cultural differences. What is important is that your choices are based on a clear understanding of what those cultural differences are.

John Cutler

John.Cutler@Culturewise.net

1. Italy

The motto "Family First" reflects a traditional Italian desire to preserve and protect both immediate and extended family. Even in modern Italy, extended family and family-like personal networks provide a powerful reference point for Italians, whether in business or beyond.

Introduction

It was not until 1861 that Italy emerged as a nation state. Before that date the country was divided into a number of independent political entities. Perhaps the most pressing of the many challenges facing Italy in 1861 was the need to bring a sense of cohesion to a politically, geographically and economically disparate emerging nation.

To some extent today's Italy is still characterised by a complex web of conflicting political, social and economic divisions. The most obvious of these divisions is between the highly industrialised north of the country and the less developed south, known as the *mezzogiorno*. These two halves of Italy hold some distinctly different attitudes to life and business. In broad terms people in northern Italy tend to follow an approach to business reminiscent of that found in many northern European countries, while in the South the lifestyle runs along similar lines to Mediterranean countries. Despite these differences, there are some common cultural themes that remain true for most of Italy's diverse regions. These themes relate to family, networks, status and the importance of retaining the respect of, and influence with, other people.

The cultural background to business in Italy

La Famiglia

In the absence of a strongly cohesive national identity, family life remains a central focus of Italian society. Indeed many Italians tend to identify with their extended families, local villages and home towns more than with their regions or indeed their country.

The function of *la famiglia* in Italy is, however, somewhat different to that found in Anglo-Saxon cultures. The traditional Italian extended family provides its members with the services of an unofficial job placement agency, financial support in times of economic difficulty, and informal support network that protects against a whole range of undesirable events. The Mafia, at least in its original expression, can be seen as a deviated form of extended family: a personal, collective and economic establishment founded on a strong network of mutual obligations and guarantees. At the centre of the familial universe, around which everything rotates, stands the Italian mother. Her role is essential. She maintains a watchful eye over the members of her family and provides a lifelong unifying reference point.

With increased affluence it might have been expected that close family relationships would have declined in importance. In fact, recent research on the family in Italy indicates that its value as a support network is increasing rather than diminishing. In contrast with many other parts of Europe, the number of children who continue to live with their parents beyond the age of 30 has gone up steadily over the last few years.

The deeply held Italian cultural belief in mutual family and group responsibilities has powerful echoes in the social relationships that shape Italian business. Business people generally prefer to deal with contacts they know, even if their acquaintance is based on a brief meeting at a trade fair or an introduction from someone they trust. Corporate power structures in Italy are, like those in much of the world, multi-layered. But in Italy in addition to the normal vertical lines of corporate decision-making, traditional companies often have a parallel horizontal power structure based on personal, reciprocal networks. This *Cordata* (which describes a team of mountain climbers on the same rope) means that the most important layers at which decisions are made may be those farthest from the public eye. Most *Cordata* are based around one person, usually a man, who builds alliances based on his personal relationships and connections. These alliances provide strong informal communication networks through which important information can travel very rapidly to everyone in the company who really matters.

The *Cordata* concept can be difficult to fully explain to outsiders. But it exists and can make the true decision-maker in an organisation hard to single out, partly because he may not be obvious from the visible organisational structure.

Given the persistence of the *Cordata* it is perhaps unsurprising that the long-standing Italian custom of seeking favours from people in power continues. The process of *raccomandazione* uses friendships, both political and personal, to seek favours in business and beyond. Surveys continue to suggest that in some sectors the best way to get a job is not just by merit, but also often through *raccomandazione*. Although this may be seen as influence peddling or corruption in other cultures (as it often is in Italy) it remains a continuing fact of business life.

'Good' people

The Roman Catholic Church and its beliefs and practices have had a profound influence on Italian culture and self-understanding. Until the 13th century there was no concept of Purgatory in Catholic tradition. The Church invented *Purgatorio* as a third place that exists somewhere between *Inferno* (hell) and *Paradiso* (paradise). *Purgatorio* was seen as a state between life and death where the living could pay Indulgences to redeem dead souls. The Church created a trade in these Indulgences and amassed vast fortunes in some of the very first banks in the world. The value of Indulgences was based on the core belief that human nature is basically innocent. Only circumstances make individuals guilty of sin and, however bad the sin, the human condition of innocence is never completely extinguished.

This concept of basic human virtue has persistent echoes in Italy's own self-perception. The image of a caring and loving country and the civic values of tolerance and pluralism are well-established at all national levels, as well as in the business world. An entire repertoire of Italian stereotypes reflects a national self-view of Italians as 'good' people. These stereotypes include the merciful Captain Corelli-style Italian soldier; peasants who feed and host the enemy; and the ubiquitous hospitality of the Italian table that is always open to guests.

At the individual level these self-perceptions manifest themselves somewhat paradoxically. There is firstly a desire to be oneself and to be true to one's own individual nature, reflected in the value attached to living a day-to-day life that is rich in small but important personal pleasures. These pleasures range from spending time with friends and family, to the enjoyment of good food and wine, and the pride Italians often feel in their artistic and cultural heritage. Mass consumerism in Italy is tightly connected with the appreciation and the importance of personal pleasures. Style and quality are looked for in even the most mundane of daily objects and consumers will often research potential purchases in great detail.

Fashionable and attractive clothes are particularly highly valued as an expression of individuality and personal pleasure.

The concept of enjoying small daily moments of pleasure is paralleled by a powerful need for social approval and group acceptance, and the stoical, even fatalistic, expectation that there are many unexpected events in life that you simply have to accept no matter what. 'Good' people are naturally expected to behave with a sense of modesty, respectability and formality, even in the face of adversity. Your reputation is important and your actions must always (at least on the surface) be seen as right. Putting on a good performance and presenting oneself in a favourable light is known as *la bella figura*. Behaving appropriately, showing loyalty to family members and personal networks, and respecting friends and neighbours contributes to *la bella figura*. The Italian attachment to style can also been seen within the context of *la bella figura*, with consumer purchasing decisions based on the need for acceptance and the desire to gain emotional approval as much as purely functional need.

Building relationships

In general terms it remains true that Italians prefer to do business with even superficial acquaintances than with people they do not know. Initially at least it can help to find a well-connected third-party contact to make introductions for you with the right people in the right companies. Once introductions have been made, be prepared to invest time getting acquainted and building trust before getting down to business.

Entertaining plays an important role in establishing relationships. Business lunches and dinners provide useful opportunities for relationship building and you should accept as many invitations of this type as you can. Status is important and Italians may prefer to do business with individuals perceived to be at higher levels in the organisation. With this in mind consult with Italian counterparts before extending any invitations as it is important to invite individuals with the right connections, or at the right level in the *Cordata*.

Business lunches are more common than dinners, which generally involve smaller numbers. Dinner tends to be served late: 8 or 9 pm in the north and as late as 10 pm in the south. Almost all lunches and dinners will be in restaurants and you should consider it something of an honour if you are invited to a contact's house or apartment. Wait until your contact brings up the subject of business, and if you have to talk business at lunch make sure you warn your contacts in advance. Women who host male guests should consider making payment arrangements with the restaurant in advance. Refrain from drinking too much alcohol.

Gift giving is generally not part of Italian business culture, although small gifts are acceptable as a gesture of thanks for making appropriate introductions or for social occasions. As a courtesy you might wish to think about translating one side of your business card into Italian although this is not essential. It is sensible to include educational qualifications and your full title or position as this enables your business contacts to understand your place within the company hierarchy.

Making the right impression

The concept of *la bella figura* has important implications for the business world. Dressing well, using language in an elegant, sensitive and fluent manner, and adopting the right level of formality are all likely to contribute to developing and maintaining a positive image.

Business dress tends to be somewhat more formal that in Anglo-Saxon cultures both in business and social situations. Men should wear good quality darker suits while businesswomen should choose simple but elegant clothes of obvious quality. Very informal clothes such as jeans or t-shirts are unlikely to be suitable in any business context.

Although Italy still boasts a huge diversity of regional dialects, accents and languages, the dominance of Italian as a shared language forms one of the foundations of national consciousness. Italian communication styles tend to be articulate, expressive and lucid, with inventiveness, imagination and intelligence highly prized. Verbal dexterity and the ability to express your ideas clearly and fluently are likely to create a good impression with contacts. Anticipating and learning to deal with interruptions is also likely to prove a useful skill. In larger international organisations and among younger generations English is widely spoken. However, in smaller organisations take care to find out the level of English spoken by counterparts and be careful not to overestimate it. If in doubt use an interpreter. Regardless of the level of English spoken by your contact, learning and using some Italian can be useful in creating the right impression. Product information or business literature should almost always be translated into Italian.

Formalities of all types are valued. Professional titles are commonly used and you should make an effort to find out and use your contacts' titles. Anyone who has graduated from university is a *Dottore*. Engineering graduates are called *Ingegnere*. Lawyers are addressed as *Avvocato* (men), or *Avvocata* (women). Many Italians also continue to use their colleagues' surnames until invited to move to a first name basis. While there is a certain level of tolerance extended to foreigners you should check with your contacts about what is appropriate in the company you are dealing with. If in doubt use *Signore* (Mr) or *Signora* (Mr) plus the family name, rather than first names. Greetings tend to follow the standard European fashion, although may be somewhat warmer and more effusive than elsewhere. Handshakes are standard with both male and female contacts. Eye contact can be somewhat stronger than in Anglo-Saxon cultures and failing to demonstrate strong eye contact can be seen as a sign of boredom or disinterest.

Persuading and influencing

Ensuring that your Italian counterparts trust you is a sensible first step in influencing their opinions. As elsewhere even the most carefully and cogently argued suggestions may not be convincing if your Italian contacts lack faith in your basic reliability and credibility. Try to avoid pushing for agreements too quickly. Keep in mind that the more important your deal is to the company in question, the more important it is for them to trust you as an individual.

Be aware also that your contacts may need time to persuade others in their *Cordata* to buy into the agreement. This is particularly the case in larger organisations where decisions are made after discussions with various people, not just the highest figure in authority. As a result demonstrating an obvious sense of urgency to close a deal is likely to put your trustworthiness in question, and may weaken your overall bargaining position. Once trust is established your Italian counterparts are likely to be as open to innovative ideas and sound arguments as anyone else. Proposals that represent pragmatic and inventive solutions to clearly defined problems are likely to be well received. Your contacts may also be particularly attracted by proposals that obviously enhance their *bella figura*, so make an effort to emphasise the mutual benefits and credibility to be gained from the deal you are proposing. Presentations should be informal but polished, with clear, simple and attractive themes. Maintaining honour and personal pride are important elements of Italian culture. As a result individuals from cultures with very direct communication styles may need to make efforts to avoid appearing blunt. Constructive criticism is welcomed and should not be avoided, but there is nevertheless an expectation that feedback, particularly negative feedback, be provided in formal ways.

Dealing with hierarchies

The continuing relevance of the *Cordata* reflects a concern with status and hierarchy that pervades much of Italian society. As elsewhere however, official titles may not necessarily coincide with actual responsibilities. Instead authority lies with the individual and his position and overall influence in the *Cordata*. Leaders often pride themselves on their ability to identify and exploit business opportunities without formalised in-depth studies. Instead, strategic planning at the senior level may be relatively unstructured and rely on a broad range of informal soundings taken at all levels of the *Cordata*.

In order to be successful in dealing with Italian companies it is important to develop a reliable understanding of the inside structure and real hierarchies of the company you are dealing with. The goal is to understand which individuals or networks have the real power, and then to take the time to form, nurture and maintain good personal relationships with the key decision-makers.

Of course it can sometimes be very difficult to decipher who holds power in companies about which one knows very little. In family-owned businesses it is a good bet to assume the head of the family usually makes the final decision. When dealing with larger companies it can sometimes be useful to use a third-party, such as a lawyer or consultant, to establish contact with the right people.

Managing people

In larger Italian organisations management styles tend to be fairly similar to styles elsewhere in Europe. In smaller companies the appearance can sometimes be of a fairly rigid hierarchy with little visible association between the ranks, together with clear respect for power usually centred on a senior figure. Yet even in smaller companies there is often considerable care taken behind the scenes to achieve consensus around shared goals and strategies. Even if the ultimate decision remains firmly for those at senior levels it is important to take time to listen to everyone in the organisation who matters, regardless of their official rank. Imposing decisions on the basis of your rank is unlikely to endear you to your local colleagues.

The purpose of team meetings can often be to evaluate the mood of members, test the water and identify potential areas of conflict, rather than to make decisions. Agendas are made and distributed prior to meetings but may not be adhered to as obviously as in other countries. Stopping a meeting that is longer than anticipated may be viewed as rude, and managers with a particularly schedule-conscious approach to chairing meetings may need to build in extra time to ensure that the opinions of everyone can be heard. Discussions in meetings can be robust, with frequent interruptions and parallel conversations common. Managers who are not prepared for this style of team meeting can easily get off track.

Italy has one of the lowest rates of female labour market participation in Europe, as well as one of the lowest rates of childbirth. Partly these low rates relate to rigidities in the Italian labour market which simultaneously increase the costs of having children and discourage the participation of married women. An equally important explanation can be found in common attitudes amongst Italian men. While women are the supreme authority at home this does not mean equal recognition or authority in business settings. Few Italian women hold managerial positions and although they have made significant inroads in areas such as fashion and advertising, women are rarely seen in senior positions. Foreign businesswomen may need to demonstrate exceptional professionalism in order to ensure their influence is felt in the right places.

Managing time, schedules, deadlines and bureaucracy

In the North, and especially in big cities and in larger companies, working times are those of other European cities. For shops and some smaller businesses, hours in northern Italy can still be from 8.30 am to 12.30 pm, and around 3.30 to 6.30 pm. In central and southern Italy business starts at around 8.30 am, with lunch from around 1 pm to 4.30 or 5.00 pm, and a further opening period to 7.30 or 8.00 pm, Monday to Friday and sometimes Saturday morning. Business is often discussed over lunch and it is common to use extended lunch breaks to consolidate the personal networks that drive much of Italian business relationships.

With the exception of really bad weather Italians tend to spend a great deal of time on the streets. Young people gather outsides bars and stores or in central squares, where they spend the time chatting and people watching. The *passeggiata* or 'Main Street walk' refers to relaxed walks taken by families or friends, the purpose of which is simply to chat and socialise.

Broadly speaking strict punctuality in southern Italy is given less importance than elsewhere, particularly in the public sector. Nevertheless business visitors should always arrive on time and fully prepared for meetings. Generally the best times to schedule appointments are between 10 and 11 am, and after 3 pm. As in much of continental Europe, many smaller firms are closed throughout August.

2. Belgium

According to a recent comment by a senior Belgian politician, Belgium is an "accident of history with no intrinsic value". Possibly so, but Belgians also happen to live in one of the most economically and socially successful nation states in Europe.

Introduction

Belgium's population of approximately ten million is divided between two distant, unsympathetic, and sometimes distinctly acrimonious regions. Flanders, located in the northern part of the country adjacent to the Netherlands, contains around five and a half million Dutch or 'Flemish' speakers. In the South, closest to France, lies Wallonia with around three and a half million French speakers. In the centre is Brussels; officially bilingual but in reality dominated by French-speakers. A small number of German speakers also live in the eastern region.

Any attempt to understand modern Belgian culture therefore begins with a simple question: how is it that from the Middle Ages onwards the provinces, counties and duchies that comprise this quarrelsome and querulous country have consistently been among the richest and most developed regions in the world? Perhaps an equally important question for foreign business visitors to consider is whether it actually makes sense to talk about a single Belgian business culture at all.

The cultural background to business in Belgium

The weight of history

Belgium's remarkable cultural and linguistic diversity dates back to Roman times when the Franks forced their rivals the Celts and the Gauls to move south, leaving an early form of Dutch as the norm in the north. With the ebb and flow of history, linguistic divisions have been supplemented by religious and political rifts, while prosperity and power have shifted from North to South and back again.

Belgium's political, linguistic and economic divisions are mirrored in other aspects of Belgian society, particularly in the delivery of health care and education. From the Middle Ages onwards education was provided by the Church. With the growing influence of socialist organisations at the end of the nineteenth century a parallel system of social services developed with similar services (labour unions, health insurance) offered by the Church, the State and Socialist and Liberal organisations. These parallel structures still exist, and, although ideologies play a lesser role, they form a rigid maze of bureaucratic structures that can be challenging for foreign visitors to decipher.

One might imagine that with the rise of the European Union and the security afforded by decades of peace in Western Europe, the divisions between Belgium's two main communities would finally have broken the nation apart. One day soon the Belgian state may indeed cease to exist. However, there are several important reasons why that day may still be some way off.

Firstly, neither of the two communities is prepared to give up the economic powerhouse of Brussels, which because of its multilingual status would be difficult to subdivide into Flemish and Walloon components. Secondly, there are no serious political movements in either Flanders or Wallonia for closer relationships with neighbouring states of the same linguistic background. Even the German-speaking part, which was annexed after the First World War, is unwilling to rejoin the unified Germany. Thirdly, recent immigration, particularly to the larger cities, has created new communities that do not subscribe to the traditional allegiances to one or the other language block. Finally, in economic if not political terms, Belgium actually works very well. In recent opinion polls Belgians revealed themselves as being among the most satisfied with their life and the least inclined of all European nationalities to move to another country. Belgian workers are among the best paid in the world with industrial productivity well above that of Japan, Germany and the USA. Belgium consistently scores highly on quality of life indicators such as housing, health care, education and infrastructure. Brussels, with its armies of EU and NATO bureaucrats and many business headquarters, remains one of the most important and highly developed business centres in Europe.

It is clear that, whatever the political status of Belgium, business visitors should avoid the temptation to think of the Flemish as southern Dutchmen or the Walloons as northern French. There is a distinctly Belgian approach to many social and business issues. This approach distinguishes the people of this nation from their neighbours and underpins the country's many significant social and economic achievements.

Authority and compromise

During the last 2000 years, the area that now forms Belgium has almost continuously been occupied by foreign powers. Following on from the Romans came variously the Spanish, Austrians, French, Dutch and Germans. During this extended period of external domination the Belgian people, no matter what community they belonged to, developed a culture deeply suspicious of externally imposed authority. This was, and is, a nation adept at saying yes to external forces while happily adjusting imposed rules and regulations to fit the Belgian way of life. Idiosyncratic, rebellious and anti-authoritarian, this Belgian attitude is perhaps best exemplified by the Robin Hood-type literary character Thyl Uilenspiegel, who ran rings around the sixteenth-century Spanish rulers of Belgium. Still today Belgians regard most authorities, particularly their elected government, with a healthy measure of distrust.

Amplified by linguistic and political division this dislike and distrust of imposed authority has left Belgium with an intense aversion to force as a means of resolving conflict, and a corresponding attachment to compromise as a way of solving disputes. With so many differences, contradictions and historically sensitive issues, the only way for Belgians to maintain a peaceful co-existence was, and still is, through compromise. The Belgian political system, perhaps more than any other in Europe, is based on discussion and cooperation between different interested parties without a clear imposition of centralised control. All of this means that the Belgians are acknowledged masters at reaching compromise and can show a remarkably pragmatic approach in finding peaceful solutions to conflict. Rules and regulations can on occasion appear to be taken less than seriously. The expression 'Belgian compromise' describes a resolution typically reached through discussions in which intricate problems are resolved by conceding something to every party concerned.

Of course, 'compromise in all things' is a cultural value that does not necessarily appeal to all cultures or individuals. The horse-trading reputation of the European Commission, the EU's administrative body, is seen by some as an exemplar of everything that is wrong with the European Union. Some say that the unparalleled ability of the EU to arrive at agreements so complicated that nobody completely understands them or their implications is, at heart, Belgian.

In the business world what the Belgians perceive as a sensible rejection of dogmatism can sometimes come across to others as a laboured approach to decision-making and a resistance to radical change. In reality this is somewhat unfair. Although Belgian business culture can sometimes be justifiably criticised for failing to take risks or seize the initiative, Belgian businesspeople can also display a parallel attachment to open-mindedness, hard work and self-discipline. Foreign business visitors with structured and well thought out ideas are likely to be listened to. This is particularly the case in Brussels, home to a large number of global corporations and a highly cosmopolitan commercial environment.

Modesty

The cynicism towards government, the lack of patriotism, and the unstructured way of doing things might lead some visitors to believe that life in Belgium is disorganised. In fact, while Belgians dislike externally imposed discipline, whether from managers, bureaucracy, ideology or religion, self-discipline is strongly admired. In place of the assertive self-belief of some Anglo-Saxon corporations Belgian culture values modesty and restraint.

At work this modesty can be apparent in a genuine openness to new ideas and influences (providing they are supported by sound arguments) and a refreshing lack of stubbornness. Belgians rarely insist on their particular point of view and Belgium possesses one of the least nationalistic of all European cultural identities. The rather cynical old English parlour game of "name ten famous Belgians" (the list mostly peters out after Magritte, Tintin and Hercule Poirot) reflects an admirable Belgian dislike of overt national symbols. There may well be few famous Belgians, but there are equally few Belgians telling other people how they should or should not behave.

The good life

With their aversion to authority Belgians tend to be fairly relaxed and good-natured in their relationships with others. Although a certain reserve or introversion can sometimes be noted in contacts with other people, this is more to do with the Belgian respect for privacy than any lack of sociability.

Belgian counterparts are as likely to be sincere, warm and friendly as anyone else in Europe once you get to know them.

To savour life is something of a serious consideration in Belgium. *Gezellig* is a Dutch word that is hard to translate into English. It means 'cosy' or 'homey', sometimes 'pleasant' or 'fun', and refers to "the good life": nice food and drink and the enjoyment of good company. Sitting outside in front of a café, drinking beer with a few friends and watching the world go by is *gezellig*.

Gezellig is also reflected in an absence of pomposity. Humour may be used in business far less frequently than in countries such as the UK and Ireland, but this has more to do with modesty than any inherent seriousness. Behaviour that comes across to Belgians as wanting to excessively impress others with achievements or to convince others of their point of view is unlikely to make a good impression. In fact Belgian society emphasises the notion that everybody has the right to be taken seriously. The opportunity to receive a good education and a decent standard of life is a key cultural theme. Arrogance, boastfulness, or the status-conscious elitism seen in Belgium's neighbour France, should be avoided at all costs.

Building relationships

As a general rule of thumb it is important to get to know counterparts before proceeding with business of any kind. However mutual respect is a prized commodity. Modesty and deference for others means you should avoid appearing too informal as respect lost through casual or overly familiar attitudes can be difficult to regain. Instead find out the general level of formality your clients or contacts feel comfortable with and mirror this.

For foreign business visitors, savouring the good life with Belgian contacts through cosy and warm social contacts at lunch or dinner can be an essential (and pleasant) way to build relationships. Avoid talking too much shop or presenting serious issues during business lunches and if it is essential to do so warn your contacts in advance.

It is probably a good idea to have business cards translated with one side in English and the other in French or Dutch depending on the main language of the region that you are visiting. The exchange of gifts in business is not a standard Belgian practice.

Making the right impression

As has been made clear linguistic divisions in Belgium are a sensitive subject. The first rule of thumb in making the right impression is to find out the cultural and linguistic background of your contacts before using French or Dutch to address them. If you are unsure about the background of your contacts, or are dealing with a mixed group, then stick to English which is generally spoken well throughout the whole country. You can usually tell whether a company is Flemish or Walloon by the initials after its name: the former are NV or BVBA while the latter are either SA or SPRL.

As elsewhere when using English with non-native speakers it makes sense to avoid using slang and colloquial language and to keep sentences short and simple. Build in plenty of opportunities for your contacts to ask questions and clarify language they may find challenging. Follow up meetings with written confirmation where appropriate.

Take care when using first names. Although it is becoming more common to use first names at work this practice remains rare when there is a distinct difference in age or position and when dealing with obvious outsiders such as suppliers or clients. It has been suggested that Flemish Belgians are more likely to move to the use of first names more quickly than Walloons, although this is not always the case. Flemish Belgians use the courtesy titles *Mijnheer* (Mr), *Mevrouw* (Mrs) or *Juffrouw* (Miss), followed by the last name only. French-speaking Belgians use *Monsieur* (Mr), and *Madame* (Mrs). The use of *Mademoiselle* (Miss) is becoming rarer in a business environment. If you do not know where your counterparts are from, stick to the English titles of Mr, Mrs or Ms followed by the surname.

Do not be shy of shaking hands. Rather like their French neighbours, Belgians tend to shake hands with everyone in the room when arriving and leaving. When visiting a Belgian office make a point of shaking hands with everyone, including administrative staff. Men are still expected to stand when meeting and greeting women and should wait for women to extend their hands before offering theirs.

Dress appropriately. Casual attire can be seen as an indication that you are not serious or respectful. Smart casual is more likely to be smart than casual, but obvious high fashion can be seen as lacking in modesty. Men should wear dark suits, white shirts, silk ties, and conservative shoes.

Simplicity and elegance is standard for women. Jewellery and accessories should be discreet.

Persuading and influencing

The Belgian attachment to compromise means that great importance is given to the discussion of issues and the airing of opinions and also to reaching decisions through a slow process of working towards an accommodation that meets the needs of all parties. Avoid pushing too hard for quick decisions. Although empirical evidence, facts and data are important in influencing decisions, business people who demonstrate empathy and willingness to compromise are likely to be well regarded. The decision-making process needs to take into account even apparently peripheral concerns.

That said it is important not to underestimate Belgian openness to new ideas. Provided you have a strong business case you will find a wide range of proposals or suggestions will be open to discussion. It is simply that the most persuasive solutions for Belgian business contacts tend to be those that come across as realistic, practical and common sense solutions to manifest problems.

Dealing with hierarchies

In Wallonia the business culture may be slightly more hierarchical than in Flanders; however, Belgium is generally not a status-conscious country. Opinions, even from employees with no particular expertise in the issue at hand, are generally invited and listened to. Open-plan offices are less common in Belgium than elsewhere. Knock and wait before opening a door. Maintaining privacy can also mean keeping important information confidential. Anglo-Saxon-style transparency in business is not generally part of the Belgian tradition.

Managing people

Belgians tend to be firm believers in practical or common sense management styles. It is nevertheless important to avoid appearing inflexible. In the land of compromise the appearance of excessive obstinacy is unlikely to motivate staff. Visitors from less compromise-focused nations can perceive the Belgian need to disseminate and exchange information as somewhat unproductive and certainly time-consuming. In reality these processes are vital in ensuring employees feel included in the decision-making process. In meetings, confrontation is generally avoided; indeed there can sometimes be a somewhat British-style aversion to 'rocking the boat'.

Foreign managers on assignment to Belgium are unlikely to benefit from an attempt to impose change overnight or without appropriate consultation. Take an inclusive approach to management combined with clear views on direction and goals and attempt to maintain and develop group harmony. Managers from Anglo-Saxon cultures who try to influence through argument or playing the devil's advocate may well need to adapt their approach to get the desired results.

Managing time, schedules, deadlines and bureaucracy

Be on time and respect privacy. Belgians tend to expect punctuality and lateness may not be understood. Public transport is efficient and well funded but the traffic in and around Brussels can be very heavy so allow plenty of time if travelling by car. Breakfast meetings are rare and for the most part the preferred times to arrange appointments are mid-morning and mid-afternoon. As in much of Europe, August is not a great time to do business. Office hours are generally 8.30 am to 5:30 pm with an hour or so for lunch. Senior people tend to work longer hours.

3. France

The rooster has been a symbol of the French nation since Renaissance times. During the First World War the rooster came to symbolise a powerful French self-image of a superior, self-confident, spirited and forward-looking country. Many of these perceptions still underpin attitudes in French business.

Introduction

France is not only the largest country in Europe, but also one of the continent's most diverse. Bordered by seven countries, crossed by five chains of mountains and exposed to continental, Mediterranean and Atlantic climates, France is composed of a range of regional and ethnic identities, each with their own particular *joie de vivre* characterised by cultural and historic differences.

French geographical diversity is accompanied by huge cultural diversity and a society which thrives on apparent contradictions; technological modernism co-exists with a sometimes semi-feudal approach to status and hierarchy; a highly individualistic culture thrives in the most centralised state in Europe; while a hugely egalitarian society boasts some of the most elitist educational institutions in the world. All of this diversity and contrast combine to make France one of the most challenging and surprising business cultures in Europe. As elsewhere, in order to do business effectively in France business visitors need to understand when and how to adapt to local expectations and conditions.

The cultural background to business in France

The State

From the 16th century onwards, the French state's response to the national patchwork of regional diversity (and the very real threats posed by its many land and sea neighbours) was to continuously consolidate power at the centre. Decisive leaders were expected to implement rational policies through a powerful central government that explicitly discouraged the recognition of ethnic, religious or cultural differences in favour of French unity. Despite recent decentralisation and a growing recognition that there are many different ways of being French, still today the French Republican state occupies a power and position in French life very different from that of other European countries.

Perhaps the most powerful symbol of the power and role of the French state is Marianne, the icon of the French Republic. Featured on every coin or stamp she embodies the 'freedom and generosity' of the state and its many-faceted role as universal carer, protector, regulator, instigator of progress, and all round provident guarantor of the common good. There is no notion of 'Act of God' in French insurance contracts. Things in France are not supposed to simply 'happen'. If things happen it is either because they have been designed to happen, or because there has been an unanticipated combination of factors that has given rise to an (usually unwelcome) event. The entity that more often than not 'designs' things to happen in France is the state. Unsurprisingly, if things go wrong, it is the state that most often gets the blame.

For Anglo-Saxons, brought up in cultures influenced by Adam Smith and his invisible hand of fate, the strong French attachment to the role of a powerful centralised authority can be surprising. The underpinning assumption of many French enterprises is that the state should take responsibility for a much wider range of actions than in other countries.

These entrenched cultural attitudes towards the nature and location of power have a number of echoes in French business. Firstly, many companies expect the state, via the education system, to release onto the job market people who are already trained and fully operational. The widespread tendency for Anglo-Saxon companies to develop extensive graduate and on-the-job training programmes can sometimes surprise French counterparts who are more used to working within a state-supervised system of training levies.

Secondly, there may on occasion be a certain suspicion of eccentricity in the work environment, whether that eccentricity is expressed in unusual dress, unexpected behaviour or lack of conformity. The attitude of irreverence towards those in positions of authority that can sometimes be seen in British business is less likely to be welcome in France.

Rebellion, opposition and individualism

In spite of (or possibly because of) the respect for strong, centralised power in France, there is also a parallel attachment to individualism, instability and social rebellion. The French revolution crystallised and legitimised public protest as a means of taking power. Periodic massive anti-state protests have taken place ever since 1789. The most recent of these in early 2008 saw extensive demonstrations against proposals to reform French pension provision.

Astérix, the legendary French comic character who was based loosely on Vercingétorix, Chief of the Gauls during the revolt against Roman occupation in 52 BC, is a powerful metaphor for this French attachment to rebellion, opposition and individualism. Indeed, the determined refusal of a lone tribal village to bow down to Roman authority, or even to see things from the point of view of others, has all too obvious echoes of continuing real-life tussles for power between Paris and the provinces, and more recently the immigrant suburbs, the farming and fishing lobbies, and whatever other group has a grievance against the French state. At work, this attachment to individuality manifests itself in a profoundly French attitude towards team-working. Contrary to stereotypical beliefs, French teams work as effectively as any other, albeit in a somewhat different way than is common in Anglo-Saxon cultures. Nevertheless, French team members tend to see the whole methodology associated with 'team-building' as a waste of time. Instead they often prefer to be told what they have to do by a team leader with an explicitly directive role. The leader matches assignments to people, and the individuals are then left to work towards the agreed goal. Although team meetings are considered useful ways of following work progress and assessing each participant's point of view, they will subsequently be followed by informal discussions and exchanges of specific information between team members.

The importance of hierarchy

Prior to the 1789 revolution France was a classic feudal system. Strict conventions defined not only the roles and boundaries of each class within the system, but also their prerogatives and obligations. Each class was ranked on a scale of importance from the lowest and most common to the highest and most blessed. Responsibilities were internally understood and fulfilled without having to be taught.

The French revolution brought down the entire political structure and ultimately replaced a hereditary monarchy with a representative democracy. Nevertheless, a revolution rarely eradicates deeply rooted attitudes and a surprisingly strong hierarchical (even semi-feudal) mentality still exists in parts of French society, notably so in traditional French work environments. Foreign business visitors often remark on the strongly hierarchical or 'Eiffel Tower' management structures they encounter, with strict divisions between those at the top and the rest of the organisation. Each employee is ranked by the function he or she is employed for. This function defines the hierarchical level to which the employee belongs, and consequently his or her status within the organisation and the obligations he or she has to others within the hierarchical structure. Unsurprisingly, this type of strongly segmented management structure can sometimes result in a visible divide – even mistrust and suspicion – between the people at the top and the people further down. One US writer even coined the term *management by information retention* to describe common French leadership styles.

While many of these traditional French attitudes to hierarchy are changing in response to the challenges of globalisation, traditional French attitudes towards the importance of hierarchy and status still have a number of important implications for foreign business people. Firstly, the consensus building commonly found in other European cultures is not as important a part of decision-making as elsewhere. Instead, senior managers who have the appropriate authority and status make decisions. This may mean that decision-making can appear slow as authority is sought from individuals at higher hierarchical levels. Secondly, French managers often go to great lengths to build up an informal network of personal contacts to enable them to subvert strict hierarchies and get decisions made more quickly. This can appear strange to business people from more task-oriented cultures. Anglo-Saxons in particular may need to make special efforts to develop informal connections among other organisational levels; the higher the better. Thirdly, it can sometimes appear difficult for Anglo-Saxon managers to encourage French staff to work outside particular job descriptions, or take ownership of problems that do not specifically and unequivocally fall within their remit. French junior executives can sometimes also appear more anxious to pass problems on to a superior than might be common in other cultures. Finally, demonstrating respect for the status of your counterparts and colleagues can sometimes entail acting with a greater degree of formality than you might be used to.

Elitism and egalitarianism

In a society which justifiably prides itself on egalitarianism the question arises as to how talented individuals can gain access to the highest status roles within an organisation. In France, to a greater extent than many other cultures, access is based on educational qualifications. In particular the ruthless and elitist selection that takes place during French secondary education is specifically designed to enable the top people to enter the best universities, and from there to a management fast-track. In egalitarian France, unlike in the UK, educational success is not biased in favour of those from higher social classes. There is little kudos attached to attendance at private schools and entrance to higher education is free, with the exception of the top business schools. In addition, French education ascribes the highest academic status to the development of scientific and mathematical knowledge, the type of learning that is, at least in theory, less likely to be restricted to those from advantageous social backgrounds.

French attitudes towards egalitarianism and elitism have a number of important implications for foreign business people. Firstly, they need to be aware that in business, to a much greater extent than in many other cultures, the degree you hold and the institutions that delivered your degree remain fundamentally connected with your later status at work. While the worst of the French 'old-boy' system is thankfully passing away, it remains the case that gaining the right degree at the best universities (known as *les grandes écoles)* is still the most reliable way of getting to the top. Be aware that leadership credibility in traditional French businesses is earned not so much by one's actions in a position as by the fact that one has advanced to that position in the first place. Do not be surprised therefore if you encounter individuals at senior positions without much relevant work experience, as they may have been hired for their educational achievements.

This approach to management is something of a double-edged sword for French companies. Weak and incompetent leadership can create extreme conflict in French companies. If the boss makes a wrong decision this can turn into a major catastrophe as there may be few individuals willing or able to challenge bad decisions. On the other hand, talented leaders have the freedom to focus on long-term planning and results. Furthermore traditional French managers, particularly those at senior levels, can also usually count on a very influential informal network to help them to get things done.

French logic

Schooling at all levels in France tends to focus on the transfer of information from teacher to students; essentially a one-way process.

French education favours the presentation of knowledge in a way that favours deductive reasoning: first, the abstract and theoretical framework is established and then specific cases are used as illustration. Logic and clarity are stressed. This leads many graduates of the French education system to adopt a similar way of analysing situations or issues. In practice this means an exhaustive consideration of all possible perspectives before arriving at a logical and coherent conclusion. The counterpart of the Anglo-Saxon business need for a plan that works in practice can sometimes appear to be the customary French response: *'It may work in practice, but does it work in theory?'*

Rational as this approach may seem to the French it can sometimes come across to visiting businesspeople, particularly those from Anglo-Saxon cultures, as convoluted debate without pragmatism or clear conclusions. This sense of endless debate is compounded by the relative sophistication of the French language. The French strive for accuracy in choosing the right word when they speak, in order to be able to explain their ideas with precision.

Several important implications follow from common French beliefs about what is logical and rational. Firstly, overseas business visitors need to be aware that decisions perceived as being imposed without a suitable level of consultation may encounter fierce resistance. Those who complain of French meetings that 'never get anywhere' are missing the point. Consensus building is rarely part of decision-making in France. The purpose of many meetings is not actually to come to decisions, but to ensure that feelings, ideas and opinions are expressed and listened to. The real decisions are likely to be made outside the meeting by the senior manager in charge.

Secondly, the French affinity for debate and the desire to fully express feelings and opinions can sometimes come across to foreign business people as direct and straightforward, even to the point where it can appear both tactless and aggressive. Interruptions can appear excessive and tempers can be lost. In reality, none of this is usually aimed at being deliberately disrespectful, but rather simply at testing the strength of the case you are making.

Thirdly, there is a commonly held perception of France as possessing a somewhat risk-averse national business culture. In fact, the best of French businesses are anything but risk-averse. However, there is certainly a desire to explore thoroughly all possible sides of an argument and a hesitancy to make decisions on the basis of what might be called excessive intuition.

Building relationships

Most of the challenges posed in understanding and adapting to French business culture can be overcome provided the necessary personal relationships are in place. As a general rule of thumb it is important to get to know contacts and invest the time to build a personal and trusting relationship, rather than diving straight in with business matters. In particular strong personal networks are likely to prove a powerful asset when dealing with conflict and in solving problems on an informal basis.

Spending time learning French and socialising are essential opportunities to develop the kind of close personal relationships that smooth decision-making and facilitate the exchange of important information. However much you may dislike business lunches, a good general rule is to accept any invitation to attend a business lunch and to think of time spent entertaining as invested, not wasted.

As elsewhere whoever issues the invitation to lunch or dinner generally pays. It is a sensible idea to wait for your partner to explicitly bring up the subject of business at lunch, although etiquette allows you to do so just before the dessert arrives. Wine is usually served with food, but there is no obligation to drink at lunchtime if you would prefer not to.

The French Language

There are seven regional languages in France – In addition to French, the national languages include Occitan, Catalan, Breton, Basque, Corsican, Flemish and the German dialect in Alsace.

The French language itself offers four different levels of formality depending on where and with whom the language will be used:

- *Argot* (equivalent to slang)
- *Langage familier* (used with friends and acquaintances)
- *Langage courant* (day-to-day French)
- *Langage soutenu* (used in negotiation and formal business relations)

Gift-giving is not a major part of doing business in France, although giving something small and tasteful as a gesture at the successful conclusion of a deal is unlikely to harm your relationship. Business cards are important and you should have a translation of important information in French on one side of the card.

French people distinguish clearly between their different spheres of relationships: family, close friends, acquaintances and colleagues. They will tend to have a different approach within each of these spheres. However, these spheres can overlap when the relationship is thriving and it is not unusual to be invited by colleagues for dinner at their home.

Making the right impression

There is a great cultural appreciation for good conversationalists in France. Individuals capable of expressing ideas in a lucid and articulate form, preferably in French, are likely to get more done. If you are using English take care not to overestimate your contact's level of competence and grade your language appropriately. Where possible, come fully prepared to even initial meetings with clear ideas and well thought-through arguments. At the very least make sure you know how to pronounce your French contact's name correctly and be aware that it is common in France for people to introduce themselves with their surname first. Make a move to stand up when a contact enters the room, particularly if he or she is at a senior level in the hierarchy.

Formal titles like Madame or Monsieur are often used during conversations with the use of first names sometimes restricted to closer relationships. Formality is also visible in other aspects of business life such as letter writing styles, the seemingly obligatory greetings, handshaking or cheek kissing, the use of the *vous* (translated into English as "You") rather than the familiar 'tu' form, and the concern for formal business dress. In a similar vein, joking is not a key element of socialising in France, and business people tend to get to know each other first before sharing jokes. As a general rule of thumb therefore you should try to find out your contact's hierarchical level and expectations about formality before you meet. Inappropriate informality can create the wrong impression and indicate a lack of respect for your contact's status. Take care not to ask questions that are too personal as French culture tends to draw clear distinctions between work and private life.

Do not be surprised if important feedback appears to go vertically and not horizontally – individuals from less status-conscious cultures than France may even have problems accessing what they consider to be basic information without going through the appropriate chain of command. Having access to information is a key source of power in a French company. Be aware therefore that you can appear odd if you communicate with what the French might perceive as excess transparency. French culture exhibits stronger eye contact than in Anglo-Saxon cultures. Take care not to misinterpret this as challenging or aggressive.

It is also important not to take the strongly expressed opinions of your French counterparts personally. In France opposition and conflict are often welcomed as a way of testing arguments and the resulting oral communication style can sometimes come across to foreign ears as very direct. This is rarely meant to be personally insulting. The best way of responding is to be prepared to lose a little of your Anglo-Saxon politeness. Interrupt, be open to interruptions, and even lose a little cool within certain limits.

Persuading and influencing

Understanding how to influence people means, first and foremost, knowing who does what and who has the authority to take decisions. Employees tend to stick to their job descriptions in France. Work roles, especially at lower levels in the organisation, are clearly defined and in the main only those who have the authority and status actually make decisions. This means decisions are often slow to come by as authority is sought from individuals at higher hierarchical levels. Consensus building, at least in the way the British understand it, is not an important part of decision-making in France and a decision will rarely be discussed by those not directly involved.

Once you have identified the right person, take time to consider the most appropriate way to present your arguments. The French have an intellectual and theoretical approach to business and may need time to express their ideas clearly and understand the reasoning behind yours. In these circumstances the best way to influence decision-making is to come fully prepared to meetings and presentations, and to spend time responding to complex and rigorous questioning. One of the reasons why French negotiators have a reputation for sticking tenaciously to their arguments, even when there is a clear consensus against them amongst counterparts, is their belief that an argument remains undefeated unless the logic behind it is somehow proved faulty.

In these circumstances French negotiators may come across as quite inflexible. If you can express clear, well thought out and logical opinions, and your argument is sound, you are likely to win in the end. Using personal relationships to reinforce your influence on key decision-makers is also likely to help. Bear in mind that a discussion does not end just because a decision has been announced. Often decisions are contested and can be rearranged informally. Expect meetings to last for longer than might be normal in other cultures.

Meetings, whether formal or informal, are often a confrontation of ideas, based on a rigorous discussion of each other's points of view, rather than a forum for getting through an agenda. Important decisions are rarely taken during meetings. Rather, the role of the leader of a meeting is to assess each participant's point of view and to allow delegates an opportunity for expression.

Dealing with hierarchies

A competent manager is considered to be a good strategist and can generally count on strong staff loyalty. As a result it is important to know exactly which hierarchical level you are dealing with. Traditional French companies often have a hierarchical or 'Eiffel Tower' management structure, with strict divisions between those at the top and the rest of the organisation. The *PDG* (the French equivalent of the American CEO or British Managing Director) often has a visionary and long-term planning role and may not participate in the minutiae of the company's operations. He or she defines the objectives but rarely intervenes in the day-to-day running of the company.

Managing people

Managing and working in French teams can be very frustrating for an Anglo-Saxon member as it all too often appears that nobody seems to work together. In fact, it is the team-leader's responsibility to monitor and subsequently assemble all the components of the finished product. Those working in teams with French businesses would be well advised to make explicit their expectations about team behaviour and values. When one particular culture's assumptions are imposed on a multicultural team by default, somebody is likely to feel aggrieved.

Feminism, at least in the American sense, has not prospered in France. This is because the French model of the relationship between the sexes is constructed around the idea of 'a gentle way of life', made up of courtesy, and a virile Gallic bawdiness towards sweet, pleasant and compliant women – there is no 'battle of the sexes' in a typical French relationship. Every challenge to the rules of this typically French cultural game has been seen as an attack; as a blow from a feminism originating elsewhere, more especially in America. Although the last 20 years have seen a significant increase in the percentage of women who work, this still remains below the levels espoused, at least publicly, in Anglo-Saxon cultures. In addition, female employment is heavily biased towards the public sector (some 60% of public sector employees are women - although only 10% in the top administrative levels).

Nevertheless times are changing. Women now hold half of all junior executive positions in the media, medicine, law and higher education sectors and this trend seems likely to continue.

Managing time, schedules, deadlines and bureaucracy

Most French workers take four or five weeks of holiday in the summer and, with the exception of the tourist industry, French business more or less shuts down in August. Try to conduct business during other months. During the rest of the year business hours are from 8.30 or 9.00 am to 6.30 pm or even later. The French sometimes perceive schedules as flexible guidelines towards a number of different potential events, and if there is not a clear, explicit and logical reason for a timetable to be kept to, other things may be assigned a higher priority. This can sometimes be quite confusing for those from more schedule-conscious cultures. It may be important to explain to French counterparts what the consequences might be if your deadlines are not respected.

4. Russia

The bear as a symbol of Russia has endured through Tsarist influences, the Soviet period and the post-Soviet transition. Russians tend to view bears, as warm, cosy and friendly. Westerners in contrast can be more inclined to see them as unpredictable, aggressive and a little lumbering.

Introduction

A geographically immense and demographically diverse nation, Russia has had to cope with enormous cultural and social challenges, sometimes with great success, at other times less so.

While modern Russia has undoubtedly shaken off the austere trappings of the Soviet era, it is still a nation in transition. There are not many in the population who wish to reclaim the perceived certainties of the Soviet period but the majority of Russians, no matter what their background, are keen to protect what they believe to be the positive core values of Russian national culture. Business visitors to Russia would be wise to develop their understanding of the nation's cultural and social complexities, as well as an appreciation of the changing local approach to business from both the Russian and the Western perspective.

Local and foreign observers commonly refer to a number of characteristic Russian cultural attitudes. Although these can be over-generalised and lacking in complexity, what follows in this chapter are a few useful starting points for understanding some of the conventions encountered in the Russian workplace and beyond, and some hints and tips to smooth your way in the Russian workplace.

The cultural background to business in Russia

Stereotypes

Business visitors to Russia often arrive in the country with some rather questionable preconceptions. This is particularly the case if their pre-visit research has been done using Anglo-Saxon resources. For example, according to one well-known American writer on Russian business culture, the experience of centuries of absolute monarchy followed by the Soviet era has moulded Russians to accept a situation in which decisions are taken only by those in positions of power and knowledge, and imposed on those below. Thus, in place of Western notions of self-reliance and independence it is argued that Russian governments promote dependence and serve the interest of faceless bureaucracy rather than the people. Within this deeply hierarchical society attitudes towards *Mother Russia* verge on occasion into outright nationalism and dislike of those who are different. This is said to be reflected in the sometimes grandiose projects associated with the Soviet period and the fact that racism and considerable intolerance of non-conventional lifestyles is widespread, certainly in comparison with the more liberal of Western democracies. Allied to these strong nationalistic feelings is an apparently illogical attachment to the certainties of the past and a somewhat ambivalent attitude towards the West.

Finally, it is suggested that Russian culture teaches that, whatever one's status in life, it makes sense to hope for the best but prepare for the worst. Toughened by generations of poverty, sacrifice, war and dependence the average Russian accepts that the majority of important events in life are simply out of his or her control. Russians, it seems, are fatalistically reconciled to the assumption that whatever bad can happen will happen. This bleak contrast to the optimistic Western concept of positive thinking is manifested in alcohol abuse, and a deeply corrupt business culture in which bribe-giving and taking is an expected part of every business interaction.

As is usually the case, broad national stereotypes such as these probably say more about the people who hold them than about the culture in question. In fact Russian business culture is influenced partly by a broad range of traditional Russian values, partly by the receding fall-out from the Soviet era and the bumpy transition to market economics, and partly also by Western ways of doing things. These influences impact in different ways on different generations, on urban and rural populations, and on those more or less economically successful. Western business visitors to Russia should never assume their Russian counterparts necessarily have (or do not have) the same understanding of business concepts as they do. It is therefore essential to understand which type of Russian you are dealing with and avoid making unwarranted assumptions about how counterparts will behave. While some counterparts may be as comfortable in a global business context as anyone else, others may not.

Russian generations

One useful way of understanding Russian business contacts is to consider what generation they are part of. Although it is something of a generalisation, older Russians do tend to carry more of the heritage of Soviet times with them than the young. It can sometimes be tempting for those from Western backgrounds to assume that society in Soviet times was wholly dysfunctional, and has remained so since. In fact the truth is a great deal more complex. If little else, the Soviet bureaucracy assured the older generation free education and healthcare, no unemployment and a basic living standard. In a society where everyone was supported from birth until death the need to make choices, take decisions or assume personal responsibility was removed in many areas of life. With relatively stable incomes, no competition and without a bottom line to protect, Soviet managers of this generation were often unwilling to take perceived risks. This led to the development of what older Russians called *Uravnilovka*: literally 'without distinction'. In any given professional field the style, manner and quality of work was not essential for the final reward.

For many older Russian employees, the opportunity to work in a secure and comfortable environment can still be as motivating as a high salary. A comfortable environment in this context can mean being part of a structured team in which there is a relatively equal distribution of rewards and responsibilities. Organisations that stress the importance of team-working are likely to be pushing at an open door with older Russian employees. However there may also be a need to rethink reward policies, as manifestly unequal pay can sometimes breed envy, distrust and factionalism among staff.

A less palatable shadow of *Uravnilovka* can be seen in the somewhat ambiguous attitude older Russians sometimes have towards professional success. In place of the Western focus on individuality and personal achievement there may be a somewhat more restrictive notion of working for the 'common good', accompanied by a belief that organisations can only succeed if others fail. For older government officials, most of whom did not benefit from the transition to the market economy, businesspeople may be stereotyped as uniformly dishonest. Given that business practices in Russia can be extremely crude this is not an altogether baseless stereotype. Although some of the worst excesses of organised crime have been curbed in recent years, there is no doubt that organised crime and corruption in Russia remain an intractable problem. The extensive use of 'gatekeeper' powers by public servants to extract corrupt payments continues, as does collusion between organised crime and security forces. In any event building friendly personal relationships with those in positions of power in Russia may be the only way of getting things done.

On the positive side older Russians are likely to be very well educated. Russian society has always attached high social status to educational and academic achievement and the Soviet educational system was very well developed. Despite many social problems Russia continues to have one of the highest functional literacy rates in the world and exceptionally high levels of tertiary education. Indeed, it is not unusual to find older doctors and academics working in middle-management positions that elsewhere would be occupied by less highly educated individuals.

Younger Russian employees are likely to have somewhat different experiences and attitudes. Business-related and management education is beginning to be widely available, although sometimes with lower standards than in the traditional disciplines of science and the humanities. Younger middle-class Russians may well have travelled extensively and are as likely to be fluent in English as any of their continental European counterparts. Unsurprisingly, extensive foreign investment in Russia, whether through joint ventures or acquisitions, has brought Western (particularly US) attitudes, values and management styles to the Russian business environment. This means that Russian businesses working with international partners are likely to benchmark themselves against international rather than local competitors. Younger, professionally trained managers with a focus on adding value to business have to a significant extent replaced those skilful in the annexation of state assets.

Nevertheless, even with the younger generation the need for mutual respect and good personal relationships continues to underpin successful business in Russia.

Building relationships

Relationships and relationship-building are vital parts of Russian business life. Without the right relationships with the right people any business visitor to Russia will probably find life harder than it need be. Socialising with counterparts plays a major role in establishing contacts and visitors are advised to take up as many social invitations as possible, especially on short trips. Russian businesses will often attach a local employee to look after important overseas business visitors. The purpose of this is partly to provide visitors with access to a ready-made network of relationships thus ensuring they stay at the best rooms in the hotel, sit in the best seats at the opera, and eat at the best table in the trendiest restaurant. It is also partly to demonstrate the company's willingness to build a personal relationship with you, often before business deals have even been discussed or considered.

What follows are some basic rules of thumb to help visitors make the right impression and build key relationships. Most are common sense, but some adjustment may be required by visitors from Anglo-Saxon cultures.

Etiquette, politeness and courtesy are very important in Russian culture. Developing an awareness of behaviours that might be seen as rude will help to build fruitful relationships. Offering a light for cigarettes and opening doors for others, and using the appropriate linguistic form of 'you' are examples of more cultured behaviour. Studied 'informality' of the type seen in some US business cultures can occasionally offend. If in doubt, be more formal than normal until you get to know your counterparts well. Make the effort to appear down to earth, sincere, and reliable. For a number of Russians email is a somewhat impersonal means of communication, so wherever possible use face-to-face or telephone contact in place of the written word. Try not to hurry things along too quickly. Do not assume however that being polite means avoiding the expression of strong opinions. The various challenges of doing business in Russia are not taboo and balanced discussion of sensitive issues such as corruption and politics is welcomed. Russians often regard feelings and intuition as an important element in coming to a judgment about others. Visitors who deliberately skirt around sensitive issues can be seen as insincere, stiff and secretive. Expressing a genuine interest in what counterparts have to say on these issues demonstrates sincerity and is likely to be well received.

Russia remains a drinking culture to an extent that can surprise some visitors. In fact, life expectancy for Russian men in 2008 was around 59 years, compared to around 75 in the USA and 76 in the UK. This statistic reflects high levels of alcohol consumption and the near collapse in state health care services during the early part of the transition to a market economy. Socialising and relationship-building often involve the consumption of alcohol and Russians are traditionally proud of the fact that after consuming a fair amount of alcohol they can still think (relatively) clearly. The purpose of alcohol in a business environment is rarely simply to get drunk, and almost never to deliberately put visitors at a disadvantage.

When Russians wish to get drunk they are unlikely to do so at official meetings. Nevertheless, someone who tries to be sober all the time is sometimes treated with a certain amount of distrust. That said, it is important to know your limits; empty glasses tend to be filled whether or not you ask for it. Non-smokers may need to prepare themselves for a somewhat smoky atmosphere.

Business dining has become popular in Russia and dinners may begin earlier than elsewhere, often around 6.00 pm. Moscow's large, stylish (and very expensive) restaurant sector offers opportunities for every type of food so take advice from local contacts on the most appropriate venues for entertaining clients. Those who extend an invitation are generally expected to pay, although as elsewhere this can be difficult for businesswomen. At more formal dinners the centre seats at a table are occupied by the most senior people present. Aim to sit opposite them. Toasting is important so if in doubt wait for someone to propose a toast before you begin eating. Be ready to hand out numerous business cards, one side of which should be translated into Russian and include your title.

Finally, find out about the specific expectations of your potential contacts and your own organisational rules with regards to gift-giving. Generally speaking, giving and receiving gifts is an important part of Russian business culture and gifts are certainly expected at social functions. Be prepared to offer gifts that symbolise the credibility of your organisation and how much the deal you may be about to make means to you. If your organisation prohibits this type of activity you may need to think creatively about how to approach this. Making explicit your organisation's rules on gift-giving is important if you find yourself in a difficult situation. At the very least work out your response to manifestly unethical requests in advance.

Making the right impression

Russian business culture tends to prefer the spoken to the written word although government bureaucracy is a notable exception. In business important information is sometimes best conveyed in person instead of sending e-mails. In particular the phrase "you gave me your word" may well yield better results when pressing for payment or for a contract to be signed than appealing to an email or letter. If you do stick to written communication be aware that the Russian postal system is notoriously unreliable and best avoided. Unfortunately government bureaucracy will require significantly more paperwork than elsewhere. In any dealings with the government taking professional advice from a qualified legal or professional services firm with good connections is absolutely essential.

Russian verbal communication styles can sometimes come across as cryptic to Anglo-Saxon ears. Be prepared to clarify where necessary, summarising your understanding from time to time. Russians tend to listen very carefully and may leave a certain period of silence after a speaker finishes. This is designed to indicate respect for the speaker rather than an absence of anything to contribute or any suggestion that something inappropriate was said.

Although English is widely spoken among younger Russians, this may not be the case with older generations. Presentations can sometimes be made in English but it is important that your promotional materials and documentation are available in Russian. Your presentation style should be simple and easy to understand. Factual data in presentations is important, as is making a good overall impression regarding the credibility of your organisation.

When using a translator or interpreter make your own selection rather than using recommendations from business contacts. If you have long term business plans for Russia you will certainly need fluent Russian-speakers in your organisation.

The general rule of thumb in Russia is to be more formal than you might elsewhere. Initially use *Gaspodin* (similar to Mr) or *Gaspazhah* (similar to Mrs or Miss) plus your contact's surname, rather than his or her first name. Smiles are generally used only for close friends. Looking others directly in the eyes is a sign of being open and sincere. Handshakes are common and more frequent than in the USA or UK. Men should wait until a woman extends her hand before reaching for it. Finally, pay attention to how you are dressed. Stylish, expensive clothing indicates success and social status. Business dress for men or women is expected for all business occasions.

Persuading and influencing

While good relationships are usually necessary foundations for business success in Russia, relationships alone are unlikely to persuade your contacts to agree to a specific deal. As elsewhere strong arguments will be persuasive. Equally important are notions of fairness, equity and mutual benefit. A good deal tends to be one from which both partners manifestly benefit.

This is not to suggest that Russians are somehow 'soft' negotiators. In fact the opposite is true. Russians tend to see compromise, particularly at early stages in a negotiation, as an obvious sign of weakness. Delaying tactics, emotional outbursts, leaving the room and making threats were common Soviet negotiating techniques. Still today unreasonable demands and unrealistic expectations can appear at the beginning of negotiations. Extending negotiations and a refusal to yield on even minor issues can be seen as a sign of strength. Visitors should respond by being patient, warm and dignified, but ultimately firm. Negotiation teams should speak with a single voice and have a leader who is authorised to make decisions. Emphasise the status and hierarchical power of lead negotiators and know exactly who you are dealing with on the Russian side. Respecting the hierarchy in Russian teams is vital if you are to maintain good relationships. Finding out the position and power of your counterparts is good practice in ensuring they can follow through on agreements. There may be a tendency to reach an agreement in principle and work out details later. Try to end any negotiation with clear results and an action plan on what comes next. Avoid shying away from conflict, but at the same time keep in mind that strong relationships will resolve problems more frequently than recourse to contracts. Attitudes towards contracts may differ in Russia from elsewhere. In particular, attempts to renegotiate contracts (usually because of an inability to fulfil a condition) are common.

It is also important for visitors to be aware that Russian counterparts may themselves hold stereotypical views of foreigners that bear little relation to reality. In the early stages of the transition from the Soviet system to the market economy it was sometimes assumed that foreign businesses enjoyed unlimited funds and knowledge to invest in Russia, together with determination to do deals that were unfair to Russian partners. Expectations in Russian business are now vastly more sophisticated but mixed stereotypes of the West remain. Do everything possible to emphasise the mutual benefits of your proposals and do not be shy in emphasising the quality of what you bring to the table.

Dealing with hierarchies

Russia's long tradition of paternalism means that people expect – and respect – a powerful leader, whether Tsar, dictator or president. Generally speaking, Russian business culture also tends to exhibit a strongly hierarchical management structure. Senior people draw up plans and set objectives. Decisions, even basic ones, need to be sent up the hierarchy for approval. This happens because on every level of the bureaucratic machine there are individuals able to stop a project. The ability to say 'no' is often the only way they have of demonstrating the power they possess. In this very status-conscious type of organisation delegating to juniors can sometimes be seen as a sign of weak leadership rather than a basic managerial skill. All this makes it essential for business people dealing with Russia to ensure they are interacting with key decision-makers at the right place in the relevant hierarchy, rather than juniors or gate-keepers.

It is important not to assume that decision-makers, once identified, are always highly competent. The basic measure of the position of an employee in some Russian businesses is the amount of trust he or she earns from superiors. Qualifications, effectiveness and experience may be of lesser importance than connections. Personal contacts are of such importance in Russia that it is sometimes more profitable to hire a person with such connections than a specialist (even a really good one) without them.

It is also important to recognise that many younger Russian businesses, particularly those exposed to western management influences, are likely to be significantly less status conscious. Moreover even in companies which are status conscious it is possible to observe somewhat rebellious behaviour on the part of subordinates. As elsewhere, understanding the particular nature and structure of the organisations you are dealing with is the key to success.

Managing people

Older Russian workers in particular are accustomed to fairly directive management styles. Anglo-Saxon principles of employee involvement in decision-making may need some translation to work effectively in the Russian context as management behaviour construed by employees as excessively consultative can sometimes lead to a lack of respect. Scandinavian managers in particular may need to temper their famously consensus-oriented management styles with an occasional assertion of power. There may be a need to introduce new Russian employees to an understanding of how the overall performance of their company is directly linked with their well-being, as some older workers may feel a limited responsibility for anything other than their own familiar tasks. The kind of public praise and reward that form part of Anglo-Saxon management practices can sometimes also be viewed with suspicion or as patronising.

In Russian folklore, women are traditionally seen as brave, smart and beautiful, while male heroes usually spend most of their time dreaming. These folklore values of strength, courage, endurance and self-sacrifice have traditionally been presented as models for Russian girls to follow from an early age. Although gender equality was enshrined in the constitution of the USSR in 1918, in a recent survey 46% of women selected "financial reasons" as their main motivation for working, while only 2.8% selected "having a career". Few women are at senior levels in either management or government, although western businesswomen are likely to be accepted. Dressing and acting professionally at all times and emphasising levels of competence and responsibility are good rules of thumb for professional women visiting Russia.

Managing time, schedules, deadlines and bureaucracy

Outright corruption in Russia is compounded by a number of bureaucratic problems including ambiguities with relation to business law, extensive government red tape and organised crime. The general rule is to take professional advice, and drawing on the knowledge of Russian colleagues is essential in handling this type of sensitive issue.

There are a number of useful hints that will help in dealing with Russian attitudes towards schedules and deadlines. Obtaining appointments with the right person at the right level can be a challenge. Perseverance and persistence are important. Schedule appointments well in advance and reconfirm a few days before the meeting is due to take place. Business hours are generally 9 am to 5 pm, although in the provinces the working day may finish earlier. The long-hours culture found in many Anglo-Saxon organisations is not particularly characteristic of Russian businesses. During the working day schedules are often subject to change, particularly if senior people or important relationships place unanticipated demands on your business contacts. Generally speaking, the more important your business proposal is for your contacts the more likely they will keep to whatever schedule has been agreed with you. While it is important for you to be on time for meetings, demanding obsessive punctuality from others can sometimes be perceived as a lack of flexibility on your part. In this vein, do not be tempted to view comments such as "we will try to get this done on time" as demonstrating a lack of commitment or interest from local counterparts. A more productive way of seeing things is to view these types of comments as indicating willingness to operate in continually changing conditions, rather than any lack of commitment to the goal at hand.

5. United Kingdom

The British bulldog: dependable, firm, trustworthy, a little stubborn, but generally reasonably amenable once you get to know him. The bulldog also bears more than a passing resemblance to Winston Churchill, Britain's renowned wartime Prime Minister.

Introduction

Business visitors to the UK may well need to set aside more than a few stereotypes in order to do business effectively with the country's hugely diverse workforce. For example, modern Britain is no more class-bound than any other society in contemporary Europe or North America, and the British are some of the least 'cold' or stand-offish people to do business with in the world.

The cultural background to business in the UK

The British identity

The national identity of the inhabitants of the United Kingdom of Great Britain and Northern Ireland is a complex issue, perhaps as much to the British as anyone else. Until the 19th century the term British did not even exist: the inhabitants of Great Britain and Ireland were English, Scottish, Welsh or Irish. It was only with the beginning of a powerful empire that the concept of being British came into common use. With the end of empire and relative loss of British political, economic and social influence, it might have been expected that the concept of being British would fade away. In fact, despite the recent extensive devolution of power from the centre to the UK's constituent nations there are as yet few overwhelming political or economic forces pulling the United Kingdom apart. There is certainly no widespread desire for political change to involve closer ties with the European continent.

Nevertheless it is important for business visitors to the UK to remember that many people who live in the country think of themselves primarily as Scottish, Welsh, Irish, English, or as a member of an ethnic minority, rather than as British. It is particularly important not to assume that the people of Scotland, Wales and Northern Ireland share the same cultural identity as the English. Addressing Scottish, Welsh or Irish people as 'English' in business meetings is, in particular, likely to invite a robust response. Equally important is the need to recognise the huge cultural diversity of the UK. In the country as a whole around 10% of the resident population was born overseas, with the figure rising to an astonishing 30% of central London residents. These figures do not include second generation ethnic minority inhabitants who were born in the UK, or the new immigrants who arrive from overseas each year.

Britain and class

Britain has long been regarded as an example of a society divided by class rather than by language or ethnicity. In reality this image of Britain is something of an anachronism. While the stereotype of a class-obsessed Englishman might once have had a basis in reality much has changed over the last 50 years, especially since the Thatcher revolution of the 1980s. In particular there has been a wholesale rejection of the need to show extreme deference to those of senior rank that was once a hallmark of the British social experience.

In reality modern Britain is no more class-bound than any other contemporary society in Europe or North America. This is not, however, to say that British attitudes to social class are exactly the same as elsewhere. In fact, class continues to be internalised in the UK to a greater extent than in almost any other advanced society. Class distinctions in Britain continue to revolve around things on the inside such as the way you speak, the books you choose to read, or the way you hold your knife and fork, rather than things on the outside such as the money you earn or your job title. This means British people themselves are often capable of detecting nuances of accent, manner and dress of which foreign visitors are likely to be completely unaware. It is this often unconscious tendency among the British to categorise others based on internal rather than external factors that has led to many of the stereotypes of the British as 'class-obsessed'.

Paradoxically, it is perhaps the fact that social class is so internalised in Britain that makes it less important for the British to use formal forms of address in business or elsewhere. Although interaction may be somewhat more formal outside London, first names are commonly used in most business situations from first acquaintance, and the British can find the use of formal titles and forms of address (e.g. *Mr, Herr Doktor, Monsieur*) in the work environment both surprising and uncomfortable. Professional titles are rarely used in conversation with the exception of doctors or religious figures.

The 'cold' British

The British have a wholly unjustified cultural stereotype as being cold or standoffish. In fact there is nothing innately distant about the British, although tolerance of others is a core cultural value. In public the British tradition of tolerance is most visible in a relatively consensual approach to the imposition of political control and a longstanding absence of political extremism. In private it surfaces most often in a shared belief in 'leaving other people alone' and avoiding conflict. For the British this often means not making potentially controversial statements in public, not imposing beliefs or unwelcome attention on someone, not invading personal space, and not assuming that people have any desire to initiate a conversation with someone they do not know on a bus or a train. In reality, provided that they feel everyone's individual boundaries are being respected the British are as friendly and outgoing as anyone else on the planet.

This desire to leave people alone and avoid conflict also helps to explain why many British people use a somewhat more indirect communication style than their European and North American neighbours. One characteristic of this indirect style is the variety of communication techniques the British use to express complex messages, particularly those that can be seen as overtly confrontational. In particular humour and joke-telling contain a complex range of functions above and beyond making people laugh. These include defusing tension, particularly in difficult or confrontational situations; speeding up discussion; making criticisms; showing disagreement; showing disappointment and introducing new ideas.

Of course, the British can, when required, be as unambiguous as any other nationality (as anyone watching exchanges in the British parliament can testify). However this type of directness tends to be delivered within the fairly formalised parameters of courteous 'debate', or relies on the ability of counterparts to read between the lines of some fairly ambiguous messages.

As a business traveller, if you think your British contacts are being very direct, perhaps to the point of rudeness, this is probably because they feel they are communicating within the parameters of a 'debate', or you have failed to 'read between the lines' and as a result they feel they have been backed into a corner. In addition, the British do not feel the need to communicate a corporate way of doing things in as explicit a way as, say, in the United States. US-style socialisation into company values can sometimes be seen as manipulative, or even as intrusion into what should be private and personal spheres of life.

British non-verbal communication is similar to other European countries, although there is typically less direct eye contact than in France or Germany. Handshakes are the norm when meeting people for the first time or at the beginning and end of periodic business meetings, but are not generally used with close colleagues or friends. Most British find the French tendency to shake hands with colleagues every morning quite strange.

The British and authority

The British have a somewhat hesitant attitude towards what they perceive as the imposition of authority. In many British companies not only is there no automatic respect for bosses and high-achievers, there is often some irreverence shown towards those in senior positions. Labelled the 'Tall Poppy Syndrome', this irreverence can be characterised as ambivalence towards anyone considered to be over-achieving or with too much ambition. Thus, in place of the 'tough' American manager, the 'elitist' French manager or the 'technocratic' German manager, the British manager tends to be chosen for his or her 'soft skills'. In this case, soft skills can be defined as the ability to communicate effectively and persuasively and gain the consent of colleagues and subordinates to important decisions.

Business visitors from some cultures may find it hard to match this view of the British as anti-authoritarian with what they view as a national tendency for conformism. In fact conformity, rather like class, is often internalised by the British. Rules, written or unwritten, tend to be obeyed without the need for too much external control. As a result excessive systematisation and the imposition of decisions without sufficient consultation will damage the standing of business visitors in the eyes of their British contacts. As the UK workforce is characterised by high mobility, both nationally and internationally, employees tend to take a relatively short-term view of employment. Intense loyalty to an employer is rarely part of British culture and British employees are likely to change jobs rapidly if they feel insufficiently involved in decision-making. Achieving consensus, avoiding disharmony and not being seen to impose decisions in an obviously authoritarian way remain important elements of what the British perceive as 'good management'.

It is, however, important for business visitors to remember that the British need for consultation is rarely demonstrated in the kind of formalised consensus-seeking systems common in Scandinavian, German or Dutch companies. Nor does it usually include the kind of formal Trade Union involvement that is common elsewhere, at least in the private sector. Trade Unions in general have little influence outside the public sector. Instead, British consensus-seeking is likely to be reflected in the tendency for decision-making to be guided by unwritten rules and traditions. Provided that you are following these unwritten rules and have consulted colleagues on important issues you can assume they have agreed unless specific objections are raised.

British individualism

While the British value consensus and not 'rocking the boat', individualism is still highly valued. However, the British concept of individuality is very different from the self-reliance and self-belief common in the United States, or the egocentricity of some Latin cultures. Instead it can be distinguished in two closely related themes: eccentricity and tolerance of ambiguity.

Eccentricity is usually reflected in a simple desire to appear different from others, whether in clothing, gardening, hairstyle or musical tastes. There may also be something of a disdain for any slavish following of fashion or social trends. In the work environment eccentricity appears as a form of institutionalised rule-breaking. Manifested in the right situations, eccentricity is often highly valued in organisations and teams. In smaller businesses in particular there may sometimes be considerable leeway given to eccentric or deviant behaviour when exhibited by individuals seen as gifted or innovative, providing this eccentricity is expressed in a lawful, polite and constructive way.

A parallel element to British individualism is a dislike of too much externally imposed structure. This dislike is often expressed in an aversion to working within a framework that is perceived as being overly systematised or inflexible, together with a profound distrust of what can be perceived as over-intellectualisation in any sphere of life. Unfortunately, to individuals from more structured cultures, the value the British place on flexibility can sometimes come across as a lack of perfectionism. British timescales can be notoriously short-term and it may feel at times as though the British aim for the easy rather than the innovative solution to a problem.

The education system

The English education system has for much of its existence focused less on imparting specific knowledge and more on developing evaluation and communication skills. Although this approach to education has proven well suited to permitting the brightest and best to push back the boundaries of science and technology, one of its many drawbacks is that it has left many British people with less highly developed vocational skills than is common in other developed countries. This is made worse by the fact that arts subjects, such as English or History, have traditionally been ascribed much greater educational and social status than scientific or practical subjects. Foreign business visitors may be surprised at the extent to which British organisations are required to provide basic professional and skills training to workforces. Many British managers, particularly at the junior or middle levels, are also less well trained than elsewhere.

British education has become much more vocational in the last few years. However there remains a certain preference for arts over sciences and for 'thinking' over vocational skills in the British education system. Half of all graduate job opportunities in British newspapers are open to graduates of any discipline and the promotion of 'gifted amateurs' to top-level posts continues to this day. Qualifications higher than degree level, unless vocational, can sometimes make employers nervous that the candidates in question are too academic and not practical enough. Of course, the British education system does have its benefits. Employees often have a highly flexible and pragmatic approach to work roles. Mobility across several job functions and businesses is encouraged and acquiring a broad range of skills is considered helpful. British managers may be less well trained, but they are likely to have a wider breadth of experience and generalist knowledge than found in some other countries.

Building relationships

Business visitors to the UK, particularly to London, should anticipate encountering a very diverse workforce. As a result sensitivity to the background and heritage of the people you deal with is essential for building effective business relationships. While the kind of positive discrimination seen in the USA is not generally part of British business culture, equal opportunity and anti-discrimination laws are both strictly and rigorously enforced. Business visitors would benefit from finding out what their legal responsibilities are in this area before they start doing business. Failing to respect the law in this area can cost a great deal of money.

Once you have thought about exactly who you will be dealing with in the UK, it is useful to reflect a little on your own attitudes towards relationship-building. Broadly speaking, forming strong personal relationships with business contacts is likely to be more important in the UK than in North America, but less so than in Latin and Asian cultures. For the British, trust is rarely assumed at the beginning of a business relationship as it might be elsewhere. Instead it is built through demonstrating humour, flexibility and a concern for following through on commitments.

The UK is not exactly renowned for its food culture although the quality of British restaurants has seen something of a transformation over the past two decades. For many British employees lunch consists of little more than a sandwich eaten while browsing the internet at one's desk. While business lunches with clients and suppliers are fairly common, many British people are not so comfortable with the extensive networking opportunities associated with frequent business lunches in continental Europe and elsewhere. Instead spending time in the pub with colleagues provides the British with their opportunities for informal networking and is generally seen to benefit career progression. While the British consume on average less alcohol per annum than the inhabitants of many European countries, they do tend to consume larger quantities at any one time: so-called 'binge-drinking'. The British also tend not to eat in pubs (unlike in the café cultures of continental Europe) leading to the unfortunate stereotype of the 'drunk Englishman' common among European neighbours. Lunch is generally taken between noon and 2 pm, with dinner between 7 pm and 10 pm. Alcohol is sometimes consumed during business lunches, although there is certainly no obligation to do so and many companies frown on the practice.

As elsewhere, it is probably sensible for female business people to issue invitations for lunch rather than dinner to male contacts. It also makes sense to invite people to lunch who are at the same professional level as you, unless you are entertaining the whole team. Coffee and tea breaks are a good opportunity to discuss work issues in a more informal setting, but there are no particular rules about discussing business over lunch. Business cards are not generally seen as an important sign of status and may or may not be handed out, depending on the circumstances. As a result do not necessarily anticipate receiving cards even from those to whom you have given a card. Gifts are rarely part of doing business in the UK.

Making the right impression

Check with your business contacts regarding appropriate business dress. If in doubt conservative dress is the norm for both men and women. Darker colours such as black or dark blue tend to be most common.

There are few taboos in conversations with the British. However, as elsewhere insensitive comments about contentious political issues are likely to cause some embarrassment. Britain has a well deserved reputation as a tolerant country with a long history of religious, political and social freedoms. Nevertheless immigration and its impact remains a highly sensitive political issue and recent terrorist incidents have caused many to question the degree of success with which the country has handled the move to multiculturalism. Tread carefully with comments in these areas. Comments about the quality of British food are likely to invite a somewhat weary response. Negative comments about the Royal Family are more likely to invite a somewhat bemused yawn than any sense of insult.

Communicating effectively with British contacts is mainly a matter of common sense. Firstly, look out for vague suggestions that are really requests. *"Perhaps you might like to think about changing the structure of your proposal"* is definitely more of an instruction than a suggestion in British English.

Secondly, listen carefully and do not mistake ambiguity or vagueness for disinterest. The British are generally much happier to be confrontational when they feel that there are others who share their opinions. If they feel they are the only ones who object to an idea or suggestion they may not say anything in order to avoid 'rocking the boat'. Consequently you need to look for covert signs of dissent. Qualifications, vagueness, understatement and humour can all signal polite disagreement with what you are saying. Silence in a conversation does not necessarily mean agreement or that individuals have bought into your ideas. Negative feedback is also more likely to be veiled or couched in humour in the UK than elsewhere.

Thirdly, learn to recognise when the British fall into debate mode and develop your own debating skills. When invited to comment directly and explicitly on proposals the British generally assume that the rules of debate will apply, and that normal indirectness can be set aside. Debate means directly and bluntly challenging the ideas put forth by others, whether these are clients, suppliers or superiors. This is rarely meant to be personally challenging to others but is simply part of the rules. Lucidity and the ability to be entertaining are also important foundations of good debate and the British will respect business visitors who can argue their cases coherently and with humour.

Next, learn to interpret the words of your British counterparts. Keep in mind that the British are taught from a young age to 'read between the lines' and draw their own conclusions. British employees often comment that foreign PowerPoint presentations (by Americans in particular) are exasperating because everything is spelled out, even when the implicit meaning is perfectly clear and obvious. Consider adapting your presentation style to avoid being too explicit and obvious about the conclusions your audience is meant to take away. Be aware also that presentations with clear conclusions but insufficient detail or data may be rejected as too much like slick and superficial marketing.

If you are unclear about what your counterparts are trying to say, ask them to clarify their comments. The British may not realise you are finding it difficult to follow them, but will generally be direct when prompted. Similarly, if your British contacts ask for explicit and direct feedback, give it to them. The British often perceive the 'hamburger' approach to negative feedback (surrounding the real criticism with soft stuff) as insincere. If you are asked for clarity, be clear.

Finally, be yourself. Time spent on small talk before approaching business issues is time invested, not wasted (although the British can recognise insincerity as quickly as anyone else). Showing a genuine desire to listen, and a polite but friendly demeanour, will make the right impression. Maintain eye contact when emphasising important points but try not to come across as aggressive. Avoid gestures such as backslapping and hugging unless you know your contacts well.

Persuading and influencing

The presence of extensive unwritten rules and a comparative lack of formalised structures in many British businesses can be confusing for business visitors. Inevitably, it means that a wider range of people are likely to be involved in decision-making than elsewhere, and it may even be difficult to work out who actually has ultimate responsibility for decision-making. Once you have found out who needs to be influenced the following general suggestions are likely to help you get the results you want.

Firstly, be open. Transparency is an important element of work culture and having access to information is not considered a source of power as it is in some other business cultures. Information tends to be shared with anyone inside the organisation and copying large numbers of people in on emails is viewed as polite, or even as a way of protecting one's own interests.

Secondly, be reasonable. The British are fundamentally data driven and business decisions will ultimately be based on logic and facts. Demanding on-the-spot decisions based on intuition or hunches can appear unreasonable. This is not to suggest that the British are particularly resistant to change. In fact, the British people's reputed attachment to tradition can be most productively understood as looking to what the past can teach us about the present, rather than a fear of the new and unknown. Rather than pushing for instant decisions give your British contacts sufficient time for a response, and make space for them to fall into debate mode where necessary.

Thirdly, avoid the hard sell. The British can sometimes perceive as boastful and arrogant what others view as fair representations of the truth and there is a particular aversion to those who promise things that cannot be delivered. Keep in mind that effective arguments are those which avoid exaggeration or over-simplification. The best sales approach is heavy on data and explicitly tailored to the specific needs of the potential customer. If on occasion the British sometimes appear to ask naïve questions, this is best understood as their way of gaining a broader perspective on the issue in question. For the most part British business people do not necessarily see the need for expert knowledge as a pre-requisite for contributing to a discussion.

Dealing with hierarchies

The role of top management in the UK is generally to identify business opportunities and persuade others in the organisation to pursue them. Similarly, British middle managers often see their role as coordinators through persuasion and negotiation rather than controllers. Whatever their role, the need for British leaders and managers to possess soft skills is always emphasised and the British are often inclined to see as interpersonal issues those types of problems that other cultures might put down to lack of role clarity or structure. Business visitors dealing with UK hierarchies will therefore benefit from well-developed persuasion and negotiation skills and the ability to communicate a strategic view persuasively.

As elsewhere, female employees dominate in sales and administrative posts. However enormous strides have been made in recent years to expand opportunities, with 31% of middle-management posts held by women. Business visitors should anticipate finding female colleagues, clients and suppliers at senior levels in all sectors of the economy.

Managing people

Many British employees consider it is more important to know what has to be done than who has the power to do it, and the burden of coordinating functions often falls on individual managers rather than centralised, structured or formalised decision-making processes. Consequently British employees are much more likely to respond to managers who demonstrate consideration, support and concern, rather than obvious drive and ambition or an overly process-focused approach.

Management 'tough-talk' is not likely to be appreciated. Instead a sense of inclusiveness and humour is more conducive to getting things done. The British are natural team-workers who perform best in relatively unstructured, free-thinking environments where there are opportunities for creativity and challenge. Building in opportunities for participation in the planning process is likely to result in less of a need to 'sell' management decisions once they have been taken. Meetings are often informal and consensus is important if individuals are to buy into a decision even if it is only a passive kind of consensus. Personnel changes are rarely political and are usually about accommodating the available talent and creating opportunities for personal development.

Managing time, schedules, deadlines and bureaucracy

Normal working hours are from around 9 am to 5 pm, Monday to Friday. While many people put in longer days, the UK cannot really be considered a long-hours culture to the same extent as the USA or Japan. It is easiest to arrange appointments mid-morning or mid-afternoon. Punctuality is expected and appreciated although in London problems with traffic and the transport infrastructure have created a certain amount of acceptance over minor lateness.

6. Spain

Following the death of the dictator Franco in 1975 a single generation has seen Spain change from a deeply conservative, inward-looking nation into one of Europe's most genuinely liberal democracies. Yet many Spanish traditions, including bull-fighting, remain firmly in place.

Introduction

In the last three decades no western European country has changed faster, or more fundamentally, than Spain. The power and influence of the established systems of authority – family, church, and state – were dramatically curtailed. Conservative, even repressive social attitudes have been comprehensively rejected by a single generation determined to see Spain complete its transition to a pluralist democracy made up of distinct autonomous regions.

In business however, the contemporary values of the 'new' Spain still sometimes co-exist with a range of more traditional cultural values and a complex series of regional and linguistic identities. When dealing with Spanish business contacts and clients, particularly those in family-run or more traditional firms, a key question to ask is *"Which Spain are you dealing with?"*

The cultural background to business in Spain

Even before the arrival of Islam in the Iberian Peninsula in the 8th century, the lands which now form Spain were something of an ethnic melting pot composed of Iberians, Celts, Goths and Romans. The Arab invasion brought with it Arabs, Berbers, Jews, as well as others from the vast Muslim Empire. For some 800 years prior to 1492, Eastern and Western ethnic cultures, affiliated to Catholicism, Judaism and Islam, co-existed in one limited geographic area in relative peace and harmony.

Today, perhaps more so than ever it is important not to assume that Spain shares a uniform and homogeneous national culture. Modern Spain is comprised of 17 relatively autonomous communities, each of which enjoys some degree of self-government. Considerable political tensions and rivalries exist between the Spanish central government and the most independent-minded of these provinces, Catalonia and the Basque Country.

Spanish regionalism manifests itself most visibly in the fierce pride attached to local languages and cultural traditions. Indeed, a quarter of Spaniards speak a language in addition to (occasionally instead of) Spanish, the language of Castile, of which Madrid is the capital. Barcelona, capital of Catalonia, thinks of itself as the most sophisticated, progressive and hard-working of Spanish cities, and retains in the Catalan language a linguistic identity distinct from the rest of Spain. In the Basque country the perceived imposition of a Spanish identity and language continues to be strongly contested, most unfortunately in the remnants of terrorist activity associated with the nationalist organisation ETA.

Unsurprisingly many people from Spain's various regions and nations derive their sense of identity as much from their local area as from the country as a whole. This is particularly important outside urban areas as Spain is not marked by a highly mobile labour force. In addition the last decade has seen a high level of immigration into Spain, particularly from Spanish-speaking Latin-American countries and from elsewhere within the European Union.

As a consequence of all these factors, it is essential for foreign business visitors to show sensitivity towards the regional, ethnic, generational and linguistic characteristics of their business contacts in Spain. Nevertheless, there are a number of basic cultural values that can be ascribed more or less clearly to most of Spain's regions.

Individualism and connections

The Spanish are often described as a highly individualistic people. However, it is important not to confuse the Spanish notion of individualism with either American-style self-reliance, or British-style eccentricity. Instead, Spanish individualism translates into a tendency to trust individuals over authorities or institutions. In other words, if you are an individual who is worth respecting, with honour, reliability and dignity, you will be respected. This is because you can be relied on as an individual even if the institutions to which you belong are unreliable. Your character, trustworthiness, and ability to keep your word are what mark you out, no matter how much or how little money you have, or the reliability of the company you belong to.

While Spain is a highly individualistic culture there continues to be, in some ways paradoxically, a highly communal approach to some aspects of life, at least in comparison with many Northern European and Anglo-Saxon cultures. Spanish history has been dominated by Roman, Islamic and then Catholic rule. All three forces were marked by strongly authoritarian power structures in which coercion, centralisation and tribal loyalties were of paramount importance. The underlying belief is that a person's sense of self-respect is closely connected with fulfilling one's responsibilities and allegiances to the family, group, neighbourhood or town to which one belongs. One author has likened it to a clan system. Inside the clan sit relatives, friends, political allies, and other trusted acquaintances, linked by a more or less overt network of mutual obligations. Outside the clan sit others to whom individuals owe no allegiance, and who may even be viewed with some suspicion.

In the business world the Spanish word *enchufismo* describes the mutual network of obligations involved in doing favours to other people within one's own clan. Examples of *enchufismo* range from placing associates or family members in jobs, regardless of suitability, to awarding contracts to a favoured contractor. At best favouritism, at worst corruption, *enchufismo* is still seen by some Spanish people as a forgivable (if not necessarily desirable) way of ensuring that one's own interests are looked after.

The Spanish affinity towards members of their own clan can also sometimes be expressed in a certain suspicion of eccentricity or of those individuals who do not overtly fit into recognisable groups. Most overseas business visitors to Spain are, almost by definition, unlikely to be pre-existing members of any useful local networks. As a result, whether in a crowded bar or a large company, the foreigner who is not obviously associated with any group can feel like he or she is being afforded a distinctly inferior status and priority. Visitors to Spain can of course move beyond their outsider status by making extra efforts to fit in.

Unsurprisingly, in a cultural environment which values personal honour and complex networks it is vitally important to prevent oneself and others from losing the respect of group members. Moving away from the area in which one grew up and in which one has a well developed network of mutual obligations can sometimes be seen as a symptom of desperation, not ambition. Face, personal honour, dignity and pride are key elements of the Spanish self-image. In the work environment the focus on face and pride can sometimes be reflected in a dislike of perceived criticism, particularly when delivered in public or in front of peers, or of losing one's temper or making mistakes in public. There may be a reluctance to reveal bad news and an 'indirect' approach to giving feedback, particularly if it is disagreeable or uninvited.

Creativity and improvisation

The individualistic streak within Spanish culture is accompanied by a dislike of, and occasional rebelliousness towards, imposed authority. Spain is not an Anglo-Saxon or Japanese-style 'long-hours' culture. Work is mainly valued for what it brings to the rest of one's life rather than as an end in itself. As a result being good at improvising and creative in what one produces can often be seen as more worthwhile than achieving fixed and apparently arbitrary external targets.

At work, the affinity for improvisation can come across as a relaxed approach towards formalised planning or forecasting and a desire to get around, rather than work within, the system. The Spanish proverb '*Hecha la ley, hecha la trampa*', roughly translatable as 'Every law has a loophole', describes this attitude well. From the Spanish perspective it is more important to be able to improvise creatively in response to the business environment than to stick rigidly to pre-determined (and sometimes inflexible) plans.

Building relationships

Transparency and openness of information flow is not generally a Spanish business characteristic. Business visitors in Spain should start from a simple premise: business is personal. In order to ensure extended commercial success you should be prepared to get to know colleagues and clients at an individual level. Make sustained efforts to build and maintain effective relationships and treat contacts with warmth and respect at all times.

In general the techniques for building relationships in Spain are much the same as elsewhere in Europe. Business entertaining is important, particularly business lunches. Lunches usually start between 1 pm and 2 pm and may last longer than is common elsewhere. Make sure you invite contacts at the right organisational level and take your cue from your contacts as to whether business discussions are appropriate. If it is essential for you to talk business over lunch warn your counterparts in advance and wait until coffee is served at the end of the meal. As elsewhere, the person extending the invitation generally pays. Business dinners are becoming more common, but be aware that dinners rarely start before 9 pm and can go on a great deal later than elsewhere. Social events rarely begin at the advertised time so check with your contacts what time you should arrive.

There are few taboos in conversation with Spanish business contacts. Uninformed comments about bullfighting, the contested sovereignty of Gibraltar, or the Spanish possessions of Ceuta and Melilla on the African continent are likely to receive a robust response. Be sensitive to regional issues and avoid assuming that every part of Spain is the same. Be aware that your Spanish contacts may be keen to find out more about you and your background than would be the case elsewhere. This helps them to understand who you are and how you fit in to your organisation. Be prepared to provide as much personal information as you feel comfortable with.

Gift-giving is not an important part of Spanish business although it is common to give hampers of food and drink at Christmas. Gifts should not be obviously extravagant in order to avoid the risk of being seen as a bribe. If you receive a gift, open it immediately. Take plenty of business cards and make sure you include relevant titles as this helps your counterparts understand where you fit within your company.

Making the right impression

Maintaining face, personal dignity and honour (yours and those of your business contact) are important elements in making a good impression in Spain. Effective communication takes place through spoken and personal contacts and requires time for socialising and informal discussion. The aim should be to retain a warm tone to personal interactions. The ability to be entertaining and convivial plays a part in creating the right tone as does the appropriate use of humour. Be aware that the Spanish can sometimes find the self-deprecating wit of some Anglo-Saxon cultures confusing as it is seen as reflecting a lack of personal pride. Sarcasm (however gentle) is also best avoided. Interruptions by Spanish participants during meetings indicate genuine, animated interest in the discussion rather than any desire to close off what others have to say. The need to invite people to contribute during a meeting by making space for them may not occur to the Spanish. Visitors from less forthright cultures may need to make an additional effort to ensure their opinions are heard. Even if you feel uncomfortable interrupting others, you may need to be just a little more forceful than at home in order to get your point across.

English is widely spoken in large Spanish companies and the younger generations but less so in smaller family-run enterprises or among the over-40s. Face and pride mean people will sometimes not admit to difficulties in understanding foreign languages. Consider using an interpreter and provide a summary of your information in Spanish. Follow up your conversations with e-mail summaries, although be aware that asking for written confirmation of verbal agreements can potentially come across to contacts as a lack of trust.

Attitudes towards the use of first and second names are changing fast, particularly in the cities, among the young, and among those who work for multi-national organisations. Find out from local counterparts what naming practices are common in their organisations. Traditionally, first names were reserved for family, close friends and children and were rarely used at work. If in doubt or when dealing with smaller or more traditional companies use the basic titles of courtesy (*Señor* and *Señora*) followed by the surname until it is clear that first names are appropriate. You will notice that Spaniards have two surnames; the father's first surname followed by the mother's first surname. Use both. It is also sensible to address professionals by any titles they may have, such as *Profesor* or *Ingeniero*, followed by their surname.

Gestures and body language in Spain are unlikely to pose too many challenges for Anglo-Saxons. Handshakes are common during greetings, but are not expected every time you come into contact with your contacts you know very well. Eye contact is likely to be stronger and personal space smaller than in Anglo-Saxon or some Asian cultures.

Spanish culture values the time and effort taken in dressing well and as elsewhere, dressing in well-made, fashionable and elegant clothing will help to create the right impression. Dressing in ways that are radically different from generally accepted styles may be viewed as eccentric and should probably be avoided. 'Smart casual' dress on social occasions tends to be more 'smart' and less 'casual' than in some other countries. Jeans, T-shirts and shorts are rarely appropriate at any business event.

Persuading and influencing

To be successful in Spanish business it is essential to develop a network of personal contacts to ensure that your arguments are heard amongst the right people in the right places. Your network should be comprised of those considered to be of equal rank to you, and those others who have an influence on the decision-making process. While data and facts are important in persuading and influencing business contacts, your personal rapport with those in your network can be equally vital. If others have a favourable impression of you, either through direct contact or through reputation, and believe that you are the kind of person who can be trusted, then your chances of doing sustained business increase significantly.

Once trust has been established and you have reached the negotiation stage, make a concerted effort to display warmth and avoid any behaviour that might threaten your contact's dignity. This implies using language that is diplomatic, courteous and discrete. Speaking frankly and honestly, which is sometimes considered a positive asset in Anglo-Saxon cultures, should be approached with sensitivity in Spain. Modesty is valued above assertiveness in Spanish culture. Avoid the 'hard sell' and try not to overemphasise your achievements and success during conversations as this may come across as boasting.

Finally, you will probably need to persevere in order to ensure that agreements reached during negotiations are put into effect. This may take longer than elsewhere.

Dealing with hierarchies

In larger organisations the introduction of American management methods, combined with less deferential attitudes towards authority, has led to a set of attitudes towards management that is not dissimilar to those found elsewhere. However, outside of the banking, construction and telecommunications sectors the bulk of Spanish GDP is still produced by small and medium-sized enterprises, who have relatively limited exposure to international markets and management styles. These SMEs are often somewhat more autocratic than those in Northern European or Anglo-Saxon cultures. Subordinates are likely to respect authority and follow orders without the expectation that they will necessarily be consulted on decisions that impact on them. Similarly, strongly directive leadership may be more in evidence than systematic procedures, group discussion, brainstorming and action planning. In this context promotion can sometimes be seen as a reward for years of service rather than a chance to exercise greater responsibility. All of this means that it is important for you to understand where your network of contacts fit within their organisations. Forming the right kind or relationship with the right people at the right level in the companies you want to do business with is time-consuming but essential.

Managing people

In the work environment, loyalty to an institution or 'mission' is rarely a motivating force for individual Spanish employees. Instead, loyalty is primarily to other team members or to warm and trustworthy managers. While there is often an expectation that management styles will be directive rather than consensual, such direction is expected to be given in a courteous, even sometimes paternalistic, fashion. There is an additional expectation that once a clear direction is given, individual employees will have considerable freedom in deciding how best to put the decision into practice. Thus, the Spanish concept of a team tends to be one of individuals working independently, but under a strong leader.

Managers used to a highly consensus-oriented approach to managing teams have been known to comment that the participative skills required to make this type of management style work are not common amongst Spanish contacts. Instead, the Spanish may view team meetings as a forum to express a range of ideas, from which one will eventually be chosen. It can be a tricky task for managers from some Anglo-Saxon cultures to find the right balance between directing Spanish colleagues and expecting them to conform to team norms on the one hand, and allowing them to resolve problems independently on the other. As a general rule of thumb, providing Spanish colleagues with the opportunity to be creative, in a warm, family-like work environment, is likely to prove a great deal more motivational than giving them fixed and inflexible targets. At the very least it is important to exhibit sensitivity towards your Spanish colleagues' need to feel they are managing independently.

Detailed job descriptions are rarely used in Spain and assessment of staff (e.g. through structured appraisals) is less common than elsewhere in Europe. Although American business techniques and methods are becoming widespread in Spanish businesses some employees can find the concept of formalised appraisals strange. Even a general appraisal of performance (backed up by objective facts) can take on a personal tone and be resented. Your network of personal relationships will provide an alternative route to giving and receiving negative feedback.

Managing time, schedules, deadlines and bureaucracy

There are some provincial rural areas of Spain where a very long afternoon *siesta*-style lunch break is common. This is no longer the case in the main business centres although most Spanish people prefer to eat out for lunch rather than at their desks and this can inevitably take longer than in some countries. Similarly, while punctuality was traditionally not assigned the same importance in Spain as in other cultures, this has changed in recent years. Even if it is still possibly the case that minor lateness in arriving at appointments or meetings is more acceptable in Spain than in other developed countries, lateness is now unlikely to be much more excessive than elsewhere in Europe. Any minor lateness is rarely designed to be rude or disrespectful and you should certainly always make the effort to be on time to meetings. A slavish desire to follow fixed agendas may be seen as somewhat inflexible by Spanish business contacts, particularly in smaller or family-run companies.

Working hours can vary according to the season, region and business sector. Check with your business contacts as to the hours that prevail in the companies you will be dealing with. In general avoid arranging appointments before 10.30 am, or before 3.30 pm. The Spanish traditionally take all of August as holiday. Many companies either close completely in August, or operate on reduced staffing. Avoid arranging business trips during this period. Be aware also that Spain has extensive regional variations in public holidays. Many fall mid-week and it is common to take a four-day weekend (called a *Puente*) during these periods. Check the official schedules (both national and regional) with contacts before arranging your business trip.

7. Switzerland

Switzerland is well known for its distinct German, French and Italian-speaking communities. However, it would be a great mistake to believe that Switzerland is simply composed of odd bits of other countries at the heart of Europe. There is a unique Swiss identity that impacts in business and beyond.

Introduction

The Helvetii, a Celtic tribe, were the first known inhabitants of the regions currently occupied by Switzerland. In the following millennia modern Switzerland emerged as a heterogeneous mix of ethnicities, religions, languages and dialects. Indeed until shortly prior to the creation of the modern Swiss state in 1848, each of the 26 *cantons* or states of Switzerland still had its own borders, army and currency.

With such a diverse range of different groupings in Swiss society, a desire to decentralise power and maintain consensus emerged as key cultural values. Still today each Swiss *canton* retains its own constitution, financial autonomy and administrative apparatus. This loose cantonal structure is supported by a comparatively weak central government and a considerable degree of direct democracy in which frequent referendums play an important part.

The factors that enable the apparently unwieldy Swiss approach to nationhood to work include a significant shared sense of civic responsibility and a high degree of toleration and consensus among religions, languages, localities and political parties. In Swiss business, these values are reflected in an affinity for harmony in the workplace, the importance attached to assuming personal responsibility, and a concern to follow through on personal commitments.

The cultural background to business in Switzerland

Order, formality and consensus

In this small, mountainous and landlocked nation at the centre of Europe it is difficult to identify any homogenous portion of the population that can truly be considered to be native *Swiss*. In place of a shared linguistic or political identity, the tie that binds the Swiss nation together is a political desire to remain independent together with a strong sense of order and self-discipline. Although led by members of different political parties, national and municipal government bodies are run along collegiate lines in which decisions need to be upheld by all members collectively. This system, driven not by rules and regulations but by a code of social and ethical values, has made Switzerland one of the most prosperous and socially cohesive countries in Europe, a fact that underpins a not inconsiderable sense of national pride. Even if some of Switzerland's smaller groups sometimes struggle to fully assert their political and economic influence, there is a tangible shared social belief that in Switzerland each one of the country's linguistic or religious groupings enjoys real equality. While each of the various Swiss communities maintain strong cultural links with neighbouring countries, these relationships oscillate between an affinity based on shared linguistic heritage and a deliberate distancing associated with a perceived threat to Swiss identity.

Schools play an important role in bringing the country's language groups together, as school regulations require that every child learn a second national language from an early age. Military service also has a role. All Swiss men are conscripted to the armed forces and after basic training most men between 19 and 42 serve a minimum of three weeks every other year. The importance of military service in Swiss culture can sometimes be difficult for non-Swiss people to understand or recognise. Military ranks often reflect status distinctions in business and it can be unusual to find someone at a more senior level in the military than his boss.

The military experience, at least in terms of hierarchical distinctions, is a significant model for business. Military service also creates barriers for women in business. While women are in theory entitled to equality in the work environment in practice the intangible barriers created by male bonding and networking during military service remain significant hurdles. Fewer Swiss women hold senior positions in business than in other European countries, and as elsewhere they often need to work harder than male counterparts to succeed. That said, women business visitors will generally be accepted in their own right and are unlikely to experience significant problems.

The flexibility much prized by some Anglo-Saxon managers is not a particularly strong feature of Swiss business culture. Instead attention is paid to meticulously designed systems and clear job roles. Opinions can appear conservative and resistant to change. This is rarely needless stubbornness, but can be best understood as an aversion to systemic uncertainty and risk and a dislike of taking actions whose consequences have not been thoroughly analysed.

Neutrality, privacy, pragmatism and hard work

The Swiss are careful to safeguard both neutrality and independence in their dealings with the outside world. Switzerland waited until 2002 to become a member of the United Nations and the country's relationship with the EU remains that of a free trade area. Despite the large number of foreigners resident in the country (some 20% of the resident population was born outside Switzerland), Swiss culture remains surprisingly ethnocentric with a vigilant attitude towards outside influences. About 75 percent of the Swiss labour force work for small and medium-sized enterprises and live in small towns and villages. To those from larger countries, day-to-day life can even feel somewhat insular. Indeed it has been suggested that for some Swiss newspapers, foreign news is what happens in the next canton.

The country's continuing independence and neutrality has had both advantages and disadvantages. While the rest of Europe had to rebuild from the devastation of two world wars, Swiss neutrality, combined with banking secrecy, a secure currency and low tax rates, created a hugely attractive place for businesses of all types. Switzerland's enviable political stability and status as a safe-haven led directly to one of the highest per capita incomes on the planet. Neutrality has not of course come without a price, as can be seen in the time Swiss men are required to dedicate to military service and in the nation's reputation abroad during World War I and II.

With neutrality came a respect for privacy, whether in business or personal life, and a pragmatism characterised by an acute sense of self-interest. Swiss counterparts take care not to pry into what are considered personal affairs during the course of a conversation, and enquiries concerning age, marital status, religion or politics are unlikely to be welcome topics in conversation. Famously the Swiss are also renowned for maintaining confidentiality in business; indeed disclosure standards, particularly in banking, remain a sensitive issue between Switzerland and the EU.

Swiss pragmatism is reflected in business in a strong attachment to well-defined job roles and responsibilities, and a belief that top quality training, professional competence and hard work are the defining building blocks of success. Of course, the need for an educated, hard-working and diligent population is hardly surprising in a country that enjoys an unfavourable climate, few mineral resources, difficult topography and poor soil quality. For the Swiss, economic success has depended mainly on international trade relations and the development of a highly skilled and hard-working labour force. The theory is that highly-educated and highly-motivated individuals working within clear systems of command and control are best able to provide the added-value that enables the country to prosper.

Even if Swiss industriousness is sometimes over-estimated, with fewer hours spent at work than most Anglo-Saxon countries, it is certainly the case that any hint of laziness or lack of commitment in the work environment is likely to be heavily frowned upon. For the most part the Swiss are dependable and well-organised and can be trusted to follow through on business commitments in a professional and timely manner. As long as business visitors are capable of behaving in the same way they are likely to earn respect. This is true regardless of whether close business relationships exist between counterparts.

Building relationships

Although long-term business relationships are valued more than short-term deals, Switzerland remains more of a task-oriented than relationship-oriented culture. Responsible, reliable, modest and honest business contacts, with demonstrably high-quality products and services are likely to be successful, even in the absence of close personal relationships. Unsurprisingly, socialising is less important in establishing and maintaining business than elsewhere in Europe. Where it does take place most business socialising happens in restaurants rather than at home, and for lunch rather than dinner. Business breakfasts are not part of Swiss business culture. Lunch takes place between noon and 2 pm.

If invited to a private home it is customary to bring a small gift, such as chocolates or flowers. However think carefully about giving gifts in other circumstances. Until fairly recently business bribes to persons outside Switzerland were tax deductible. Within Switzerland however the merest hint of a lack of business ethics will prove disastrous to your commercial interests. Most Swiss companies actively discourage gift-giving, so if you do chose to present a small gift, do it discreetly and ensure it is not obviously extravagant.

Business cards are important and frequently exchanged. Including job titles on cards is important as this enables counterparts to understand your place within the corporate hierarchy. There is no need to translate your cards since most Swiss contacts speak enough English to understand business titles.

Making the right impression

English is widely spoken across Switzerland and is taught at a high level in most Swiss schools and universities. However, some older Swiss business contacts may have limited competence in English, so find out the English-language proficiency of your contacts before you go and take care not to overestimate it. Where necessary be prepared to use an interpreter.

If you are a German speaker it is important to be aware also that even within the German-speaking population a variety of local dialects of *Schweizerdeutsch*, or Swiss-German, are used in spoken communication. Some *Schweizerdeutsch* dialects can be difficult for those from different regions of the country to understand, let alone people from outside the country. While a shared official version of *High German* is learnt at school, it is mostly used in written communication and can sometimes be difficult for some Swiss people to use with complete comfort.

In Swiss business formal interpersonal relationships are characterised by a general desire to reach consensus and avoid conflict. Business encounters, at least as seen from the Anglo-Saxon perspective, can be somewhat formal, and for the most part the Swiss make a sharp distinction between business and their private life. Close relationships are slow to develop and are the result of satisfactory dealings rather than personal compatibility.

The transition from using surnames to first names may be slow; however concessions are often made to visitors from less formal Anglo-Saxon cultures, particularly in larger global companies. In German-speaking cantons of Switzerland it is sensible to address new business contacts as *Herr* followed by the surname when addressing a man, or *Frau* when addressing a woman. In French-speaking areas use *Monsieur* and *Madame* and in Italian-speaking areas use *Signore* and *Signora*. Avoid using *Fraulein*, *Mademoiselle* and *Signorina* in the business environment.

Academic and professional titles are not often used in business. As always, find out how to pronounce your business contact's names before the first meeting.

When introduced to contacts say *gruezi* in German-speaking areas, *bonjour* in French-speaking areas, and *buon giorno* in Italian-speaking areas. Handshakes are common for both men and women when greeting and taking leave of business contacts, however strong smiles are generally not common. Smiling is mostly used to express affection rather than as a form of acknowledging someone.

Courtesy, politeness, modesty and seriousness are important elements of communication in both social and business situations. To business visitors from more expressive cultures this communication style can come across as detached, overly earnest or even a little humourless. Nevertheless, this apparent reticence does not imply vagueness or indirectness. In fact, any lack of clarity can come across as insincerity or even incompetence.

Business dress is usually fairly formal. For men this means dark suits, white shirts, plain ties and black shoes, and for women suits or skirts of a conservative length. If in doubt ask your business contact what is appropriate.

Persuading and influencing

Whatever else they are the Swiss are true business opportunists, more open to new ideas than their cautious, conservative image suggests. However, obvious risk-taking is rarely part of Swiss business culture so in order to be persuasive new ideas need to be backed up with comprehensive data and logical, well thought through supporting arguments. Presentations should be clear, concise and comprehensive, and supported by plenty of data. Written supporting materials should be formal, businesslike, with comprehensive background information on your proposal and company. Where possible have a printed summary of your presentation available in the local language, even if your contacts speak good English.

Swiss negotiators are likely to arrive well prepared for any negotiation, and will expect counterparts to do the same. The preferred negotiating style is open and based on problem solving and consensus. Avoid exerting obvious pressure or attempting to bulldoze through a proposal. Being seen as someone who likes to haggle or drive too hard a bargain is unlikely to be helpful to your long term commercial interests. Initial quotes should be realistic rather than based on a high-low tactic. Avoid any perception that you are over-inflating quotes. There is a general preference for follow-up agreements with a written confirmation, and in any event keep accurate written records of all negotiations as your contacts certainly will. Contracts and agreements are expected to be met to the letter.

Extended small talk is not a huge part of Swiss meetings however the Swiss do tend to be good listeners and will rarely interrupt. In meetings Swiss business contacts are likely to be attentive and may even take notes while you speak. Courtesy is valued so avoid interrupting other speakers. It is also important to stick to the agreed agenda and keep within the time allocated for the meeting. Improvisation or changing the agenda can sometimes be seen as a sign of poor planning even if new issues arise as a result of discussion. Overtly expressing emotion in business contexts is also likely to be seen as somewhat unprofessional. Language should be clear and neutral. While humour has a limited place in meetings, the Swiss may be confused by the use of too much humour in a business context.

At the end of meetings action points are important and people can generally be trusted to follow through with their assigned tasks. They will expect the same from you, so it is important to honour your commitments to the letter.

Dealing with hierarchies

Power in Swiss companies tends to combine a clear and respected hierarchy with shared decision making and consensus. Although the final decision is likely to be made by the most senior person, he or she will make sure that everyone affected accepts what has been decided. As a result senior people tend to avoid overt assertiveness, instead looking for a shared consensus through private briefing and lobbying. On occasion this can make it difficult for outsiders to recognise who the true decision-maker is, as individuals with ultimate authority tend to exercise power in a fairly consensual fashion. For those from some cultures, this type of decision-making can come across as time consuming, particularly as Swiss leaders will tend to avoid entering into open discussion if they have not prepared for an issue that might lead to disagreement.

Managing people

Generally speaking, Anglo-Saxon style *soft skills* are not seen as a particularly vital area of management competence in Switzerland. Respect for a manager is more likely to be based on professional competence than on charisma. Showing responsibility, competence, hard work and honesty will usually be enough to bring colleagues on side. Feedback can be given in a direct, clear and explicit fashion. Giving vague responses to questions may be viewed as suspicious rather than courteous, and even fairly blunt criticism is likely to be seen as a sign of taking someone seriously.

Open-plan offices are less common in Switzerland than in the UK or USA, and in many traditional businesses offices doors are still kept closed. If the doors are closed, knock and wait to be admitted.

Managing time, schedules, deadlines and bureaucracy

The Swiss desire for order and predictability is very much apparent in attitudes towards punctuality. Being on time is important across Switzerland, and arriving even a few minutes late for a business engagement might be seen as a lack of respect. In social situations it is acceptable to arrive around 15 minutes after the suggested time.

Meetings are always by appointment. Allow plenty of time when seeking appointments, as diaries fill up a long time in advance. Appointments may not be easy to make unless there is a clear business case for your visit. Avoid trying to make appointments during holiday periods in July, August and late December. Office hours are generally from around 8 am to 5.30 pm with lunch between noon and 2 pm.

8. Germany

For nearly two millennia Germany was a fragmented patchwork of small states, joined together in more or less durable regional groupings and frequently split by civil and religious struggles. In such circumstances it is perhaps hardly surprising that the search for certainty, clarity, and order form such powerful drivers of the German world-view.

Introduction

Pre-Germanic tribes have been living in the lands occupied by Germany since the second century BC. Their resistance of Roman domination helped initiate the long-lasting cultural divide between the Roman-dominated lands west of the Rhine and the lands to the east where tribal groups with their own local customs and languages remained in control. Still today, regional differences remain an important feature of German life, and many Germans continue to identify with their region first and their nation second.

Nevertheless, when German unification took place in 1871 it was built upon a well-developed sense of shared national and linguistic identity, if not a clear understanding of what Germany as a geographic entity should legitimately look like. In the decades following unification, war and its aftermath reshaped the borders of Germany, with land, people and natural resources changing affiliation with victory and defeat.

The cultural background to business in Germany

The social market

Western Germany's long period of economic expansion after the Second World War enabled Germany to develop the third largest economy in the developed world. Still today Germany is the world's largest exporter of goods, with foreign sales of German made products exceeding those of the UK, France and the Netherlands combined. Although aid from the USA, sound economic management and access to bank financing were important factors in German economic success, at least as important was the post-war German concept of the *social market economy*. While acknowledging the role of market forces in sustained economic development, the *social market economy* attached considerable power to the state's role as guarantor of the welfare of citizens through a comprehensive social welfare system. Companies were held responsible not only or even primarily to their shareholders as in the Anglo-Saxon world, but to many other stakeholders including staff, suppliers, communities and customers. Compromise and consensus were key elements in the management of companies and the belief that private enterprise should operate within a public framework became firmly fixed in the minds of German business people.

Unsurprisingly, high unemployment and comparatively low growth over the past fifteen years has led to extensive questioning of the sustainability of the German *social market economy* model. Both the German political elite and for the most part the German population have recognised a need for change in order to ensure continued competitiveness. Nevertheless, visitors from some Anglo-Saxon cultures can still sometimes be surprised at the continuing influence of the state, local governments and trade unions in business issues, and the complexity and range of market regulation. In the world of business change occurs slowly, sometimes reluctantly, and with a focus on consensus and conflict-avoidance.

The search for truth

Explicit, intellectual criticism has long been one of the driving forces of German philosophy and plays a central part in German speech patterns. In particular German culture values a process called *vertiefen* which involves the use of theoretical enquiry, statements of fact and critical questioning in order to explore the core or essential reality of a question, issue or problem. Considerations of saving face are secondary to the goal at hand, which is to discover the objective truth.

Of course, in order get to the truth of any question, the exact meaning of words and arguments needs to be clear and unambiguous. This has resulted in a stereotypically German style of speech in which precision of expression, exactness of definition, constructive criticism and literalness play important parts. In terms of stating facts, offering criticism and issuing commands, Germans are often a great deal more direct and explicit than might be normal in other cultures. For Germans, being critical is seen as a way of being socially responsible rather than a means of putting others into challenging or confrontational situations.

Building relationships

Although not a particularly relationship-oriented business culture, new business is generally procured from established suppliers so it makes sense to make efforts to get to know German contacts on a personal basis. Socialising is a fairly important part of business. Lunches are more common than dinners, while breakfast meetings are rare. It is perfectly acceptable to discuss business before or after lunch but business topics should generally be avoided during the meal. Most entertaining takes place in restaurants and it is unusual to be invited to a business contact's home.

Business cards are commonly exchanged and should include your job title as this helps your contacts understand your particular responsibilities. It is probably sensible not to translate cards into German as the use of specific German titles may need to be approved.

Making the right impression

The German language distinguishes between a formal way of addressing others using *Sie* for acquaintances and strangers and the more informal *Du* for friends or closer contacts. As a general rule of thumb Germans will use *Sie* for all initial contacts in the work environment and only change to *Du* when closer relationships have been established. Where formal relationships are in place visitors should address German business contacts using *Herr* or *Mr, Frau* or *Ms/Mrs* plus the surname. If your contact has an academic or professional title this should be used, for example, *Herr Doktor Schroeder* or *Frau Professor Schmidt.*

The use of first names and the generally informal approach of Anglo-Saxon business cultures are becoming more widespread among younger employees in multinational German companies, or those with a less traditional corporate culture. However care needs to be taken as obvious informality with new business contacts can sometimes be perceived as superficial or even lacking in respect. It is also important not to misunderstand the formal German approach in the work environment as cold or distant. Rather it demonstrates respect for the professional status of whoever your business contacts are dealing with.

Anglo-Saxon business visitors may be invited to use first names with German contacts immediately. This can sometimes mean that German contacts will use each other's first names when working in English in multinational groups, but will revert to using surnames when communicating with each other in German. If your contacts use surnames and the *Sie* form you may wish to suggest moving to first names over a meal or a glass of wine once you get to know them. This is generally more acceptable if you are obviously older or more senior than your business contact.

There are few taboos in social conversations with German business contacts. However to a greater extent than in most other countries in Europe, Germans tend to compartmentalise their business and social lives, with people from one part rarely crossing over into another. With this in mind it is probably sensible to ask fewer personal questions of a German colleague than might be the case elsewhere. Otherwise most subjects are open for discussion and personal opinions can be delivered in a robust and direct, albeit constructive, manner.

Greetings are generally fairly formal with handshakes common at the beginning and end of meetings for both men and women. Other physical gestures and body movements are more contained and embracing or kissing among business contacts is unusual. It is generally better to be introduced by a third person than to introduce yourself. Smiles are generally reserved for friends rather than clients or colleagues.

In face-to-face conversations, Germans tend to use more direct and intense eye contact than other cultures may be used to. From the German perspective this is meant to indicate engagement and interest in the conversation and should be understood in this way. In particular, make sure you meet your counterpart in the eye when raising your glass for a toast.

Business dress tends to be on the formal side with dark suits, ties and white shirts standard for men and dark suits and white blouses appropriate for women. Business dress is suitable for most formal social events.

Persuading and influencing

There are several behaviours that are likely to help business visitors prove persuasive and influential with German business contacts.

Firstly, business visitors need to convince their contacts that their word can be relied upon. The German word *verbindlich,* which translates roughly as obligatory or compulsory, refers to the importance in business of living up to the spirit and the letter of promises. The underlying belief is that an individual needs to be fully accountable for comments made or commitments given. To say something and then not carry it through can demonstrate a lack of respect for others and damage the person's credibility.

Secondly, German culture values analytic thought. While trust and good personal relationships are important in developing long-term business success, rational reasoning based on extensive facts, figures and examples is the core of any decision-making process. The desire to treat business contacts with fairness or integrity means that all relevant facts will be carefully considered, sometimes by several different people, before a final decision is reached. Do not anticipate being able to speed up this sometimes time-consuming process. In presentations the hard sell approach should be avoided. Tone down any hype and provide detailed background data and information on the proposals at hand.

Thirdly, business discussions and negotiations are perceived as being by their very nature goal-oriented, and therefore to be taken seriously. Anglo-Saxons often use humour to diffuse tense or stressful situations in discussions, or to introduce new ways of thinking around a particular issue. Germans are more likely to address such issues head-on and consequently can find the extensive use of humour in a business context confusing.

The goal of initial business meetings may be to test the credibility of potential contacts or to assess the quality of initial proposals. If your intention at the initial meeting is different make this clear to your contacts. Whatever the purpose of meetings, German business contacts are likely to look carefully for flaws in your initial comments and may appear more overtly critical than Anglo-Saxons are used to. Being open about discussing weaknesses is seen as an important step in overcoming them, and should be viewed as constructive rather than as unproductive nit-picking. Arriving prepared, keeping to the agenda, eschewing too much small talk and finishing meetings within the agreed schedule are also important in establishing credibility.

Negotiations will be fairly task oriented. German business people are often mistakenly accused of being cautious of new ideas and concepts. In fact, German culture tends to be highly focused on facts; a decision to work with a new partner or follow a new approach is one that needs to be carefully considered. Business people from cultures in which decisions are made on the basis of intuition or hunches may need to make particular efforts to back up their arguments with more facts than they would use elsewhere. Case studies and examples are highly regarded. Criticism should not be taken as a personal attack but understood as a technique for dealing with potential problems in an honest, direct and explicit fashion. Detailed contracts are likely to result from negotiations and will generally be difficult to change once signed. In theory failure to honour the terms and conditions of a contract can lead to litigation. However recourse to litigation is generally less frequently used to resolve disputes than in Anglo-Saxon cultures. Instead, in keeping with the German desire for consensus and compromise, disagreements or differences tend to be addressed as far as possible through discussion.

Dealing with hierarchies

Business visitors to Germany would be wise to start by developing a clear understanding of where in the hierarchy decisions will be taken and getting acquainted with the full range of individuals likely to be involved. Thankfully, it is usually clear who has the ultimate power in German organisations and the exercise of authority is relatively transparent. German companies tend to be more hierarchical than their Anglo-Saxon counterparts, but it can mostly be assumed that those in positions of power are there on the basis of their professional capability rather than their background, charisma or networking ability. Deference is expressed to people in authority based on respect for their proven professional competence rather than on the fact that they occupy any particular role.

While functions and relationships in German companies are thoroughly defined and documented, this is not to say that communication and decision-making processes are equally easy to decipher. Strongly defined institutional hierarchies can result in much less open channels of communication than may be found in cultures with flatter management structures. In addition, in parallel with the official chain of command, German companies often have a number of unseen advisers and consultants who exercise significant influence. Detailed planning has enormous value in German culture and the approval of this informal group of advisors can be important in providing senior managers with the assurance that every aspect of a decision has been fully considered.

Managing people

German organisations tend to value managers with demonstrable technical and professional skills who are able to provide firm but consensus-oriented leadership. Delegation is expected to be clear, concise and unambiguous and the kind of irreverence shown towards managers in the UK and some other cultures is unlikely to be appreciated.

If you want to impress a German manager as an employee, you need to possess appropriate qualifications and a clear orientation toward quality, emphasise a consensus-based approach to team-working, as well as demonstrating long-term loyalty to the company. Sticking closely to the rules is perceived to be important in enhancing reliability and is not generally seen as a barrier to flexibility and creativity.

As far as appraisal processes are concerned, employees are not commonly required to contribute to setting their own personal objectives. The responsibilities attached to job roles are mostly clear and explicit and allow for fairly direct feedback to subordinates who have not followed established procedures or dealt professionally with the tasks they have been delegated. Direct feedback is rarely taken personally as the assumption is that critical questioning by managers will play a major part in enabling mistakes or inadequacies to be identified in order for them to be corrected. When problems arise, be prepared to explain them clearly, in detail, and without emotion.

Giving compliments in a business environment can be met with suspicion as competent work does not require any particular acknowledgement; it is simply part of what is expected. German subordinates may even view effusive praise as ambiguous and attempt to decipher a hidden meaning. The emphasis on clarity in feedback means that softening words used commonly in English such as *sort of, kind of, pretty much,* and *perhaps* are also best avoided.

When it comes to meetings in Germany, the status and importance attached to work roles and professional competence make it unusual for subordinates to comment on areas that are not explicitly within their remit. This can be confusing for business people from cultures where everyone involved is expected to contribute to a discussion. Generally speaking, teams in Germany are seen as a structured group of individuals, each with specific expertise and a recognised role, working towards clear objectives under a firm leader. Content, methodology and process are likely to be clearly established. Individuals from Anglo-Saxon cultures may find that their more fluid approach to team working, in which ad-hoc groups can be formed across reporting lines, is less likely to be effective in the German context.

As elsewhere in Europe, women in German business often find themselves in lower positions and less well-paid jobs in comparison to men. The country's comparatively conservative family culture still sometimes harks back to the notion that women's role in life is *Kinder, Kuche und Kirche* (children, kitchen and church). Childcare facilities are poor in comparison with other European countries and women can still sometimes be faced with choosing between children and a full-time career. As women get better educated and more involved in the workplace this lack of childcare support has impacted on the German birth rate which is now one of the lowest in Europe.

Privacy is important. Open plan offices are less common than elsewhere and office doors are kept closed when contacts do not wish to be disturbed. Knock and wait to be admitted if your contact's door is not open.

Managing time, schedules, deadlines and bureaucracy

There are few places on earth in which punctuality is more important than in Germany. Visitors should make the effort to be on time for every appointment whether business or social. Arriving just two or three minutes late can demonstrate a lack of appropriate respect, particularly if you are a supplier or in a manifestly subordinate position.

Appointments are important and where possible visitors should try to schedule important meetings at least two weeks in advance. The best time for business appointments is usually mid-morning or mid-afternoon. Avoid making appointments for Friday afternoon or during holiday periods in July, August and late December. Be aware also that many contacts may be away from the office during regional festivals such as the Oktoberfest in Munich or the three-day *Karneval* in a number of cities in February.

9. Scandinavia

Although each of the Scandinavian nations is unique, shared geographical, historical and religious influences have lead to a distinctively Scandinavian set of cultural values and beliefs. These include political stability, a desire for consensus, a belief in egalitarianism, as well as the importance Scandinavians attach to social and environmental responsibility.

Introduction

Stretching across the northern fringes of the European continent and surrounded by unforgiving coastal waters, the land mass of the Scandinavian nations is dominated by thick forests, marshland and towering mountain ranges. The original Scandinavian peoples faced many challenges and restrictions on where they could settle and farm, as land with any agricultural potential was difficult to find and even more difficult to cultivate. In this harsh environment survival meant getting on with the neighbours and living in harmony with the land. Almost completely isolated from the civilisations of central and southern Europe, Scandinavia's homogenous peoples came to develop a range of shared cultural values that include stability, cooperativeness, and a desire for stable social structures, consensus and loyalty to the wider group. Still today the cultural values, beliefs and attitudes that underpin life in Scandinavia are characterised by an egalitarian attitude towards others and consensus-seeking as a way of resolving conflict. Nurturing, non-aggressive and non-competitive with each other, many Scandinavians value material security in their surroundings and modesty in others. Combine these values with an industrious and hard-working approach to business and it comes as no surprise that Scandinavian countries work as well as they do.

The cultural background to business in Scandinavia

The Viking heritage

Perhaps the best known historical civilisation in Scandinavia was the Viking culture that developed to dominate much of Europe from around 800 until 1100. Viking lands comprised the three present-day Scandinavian nations of Denmark, Norway and Sweden, together with part of Finland. As a result of their relative isolation from external influences Viking cultures developed in a relatively uniform way. Throughout Scandinavia the Vikings spoke similar languages, worshipped the same gods and shared many of the same cultural traditions and customs.

The stereotypical image of Vikings as pirates and raiders is somewhat misleading. Although conquest and pillage were part of the Viking way of taking over territory, the majority of the population was focused on the more mundane pursuits of farming and trading. The Viking social order had no desire to develop a strongly centralised authority or hierarchical and elitist leaders. Their society of *free men* allocated power over others based not on status or title but rather on a pragmatic egalitarianism that depended more on the nature of the task to be confronted than on the status of those involved. Society functioned by emphasising the individual's need to live and die with honour; the maintenance of personal and family honour being a necessary condition to regulate peace and order. Loyalty to family and tribe was paramount. If a man's honour was offended vengeance was not only expected but seen as a duty regulated by law (with a handy alternative of exacting payment instead of revenge where this satisfied both parties). In reality, vindictive and violent family blood feuds were rare. Viking *free men* went to considerable efforts to avoid falling into conflict with each other, instead developing a tradition of talking tough while at the same time negotiating peaceful resolutions to conflict that restricted damage for both sides.

The end of the Viking age saw the emergence of separate (often bickering) Scandinavian peoples, each looking in different directions for influences, conquests and alliances. Nevertheless, geographical isolation meant that political control over the Scandinavian territories remained mainly a local affair. Power was initially concentrated in Denmark until the emergence of Sweden as a rival Baltic-leaning power in the 1500s. Norway remained a western-looking maritime and agricultural nation under the control of one or other Scandinavian rival, while Finland was subject to Swedish and subsequently Russian control.

Lutheranism

Despite differences in the speed and direction of economic development, and in particular the emergence of a land-owning aristocracy in Sweden, cultural values across the region remained similar. This was due in part to the fundamentalist form of Lutheran Protestantism that swept (or was imposed) across Scandinavia from the 15th century onwards. The Lutheran tradition emphasised the doctrine of hard work, modesty and a somewhat serious attitude towards life. Frugality, honesty, conscientiousness, initiative and enterprise were all valued as routes to leading a redeemed life, as were respect for private property, law and contracts.

Although modern Scandinavia is thoroughly secular, the Lutheran tradition continues to be held in high regard and influences attitudes and behaviours in several ways. Firstly, the stereotypical Scandinavian is hard-working and dedicated. Financial rewards are important but so are career opportunities and the potential for personal development at work. This is not to say that Scandinavians are slaves to employment. Achieving a reasonable work / life balance is a distinct theme in Scandinavian employment law and there is generally a clear divide between work and private life.

Secondly, honesty, whether expressed in high ethical standards or the desire to speak the truth, is a key facet of the Scandinavian self-image. Known for a dislike of excessive gift-giving or any other action that can be perceived as a bribe, Scandinavia ranks as the most corruption-free area in the world.

Thirdly, communication tends to be straightforward and open (some would say blunt) and any form of language perceived as boasting or exaggerated is disliked. In the workplace this direct communication style tends to be most visible in the open dialogue that is encouraged across all organisational levels. Corporate objectives and strategies tend to be well signposted and most employees will have a good understanding of what their companies are up to and where they are headed.

Informality

A further Scandinavian cultural characteristic is a fairly studied informality of approach in dealing with others. More than simply a lack of formality, it can be understood best as the proactive familiarity, modesty or cosiness described by the Danish word *hygge*. Roughly translated, *hygge* implies not only comfortable and welcoming personal surroundings, but more generally a sense of companionship, geniality and ease in dealing with others. *Hygge* impacts on how Scandinavians design their homes, where they go to socialise, and who they spend their time with. Ostentatious behaviour or boasting are distinctly *uhyggeligt,* the opposite of *hygge,* and are unlikely to endear business visitors to their Scandinavian contacts.

Building relationships

Loyalty and reliability are particularly important qualities in Scandinavia. Establishing and maintaining good personal networks will benefit business visitors even if decisions are ultimately made on the basis of data and facts. Business socialising is fairly common, particularly going for a drink after work, while a business lunch is more likely than dinner. In general social situations are forums for relationship building rather than business discussions. If it is necessary to discuss business then warn contacts in advance or wait for them to bring up the subject. Take care too in making conversational invitations to lunch or dinner that you have no intention of following up. These can sometimes be taken at face value and forgetting them can lead to embarrassment. Service charge is generally included in restaurant bills and it is not necessary to tip more. Avoid questions that might be considered intrusive or personal.

Alcohol will generally be available in the evening, but it is much less common to drink at lunchtime. Some meals may start with a small serving of vodka or schnapps, particularly when the first course is cold fish. Toasting is reasonably common. Hosts will generally start by toasting visitors who should respond later in the meal. It is not essential to drink alcohol during a toast; either raise a glass to the lips without swallowing or toast with a glass of mineral water.

Business cards are commonly exchanged, so business visitors should bring a good supply. It is not necessary to have them translated into any of the Scandinavian languages.

Making the right impression

The Scandinavian affinity for honesty and directness in communication generally makes them easy people for Anglo-Saxons to deal with. English is often spoken very well. Generally speaking Scandinavians will speak clearly and concisely and will expect others to do the same. Opinions are expressed in a direct and candid manner without the type of diplomatic and ambiguous language used in other cultures where saving face is considered important. Promises are taken seriously and business visitors will be expected to keep both to the spirit and the letter of agreements.

Be aware however that this relaxed and direct communication style can mask some potentially challenging aspects of communication in Scandinavia. Firstly, small talk is a skill which Scandinavians and in particular the Finns are notoriously lacking. As Bertolt Brecht once remarked, the Finns have an almost unique talent for *keeping silent in two languages.* It is not just that small talk is not particularly valued, it can also sometimes be considered suspect simply by definition. Rather than putting Scandinavians at ease, unanticipated small-talk can come across as puzzling and even pompous. The reaction to what is perceived as excessive and directionless chit-chat may be one of withdrawal rather than engagement.

Secondly, business visitors from English-speaking cultures need to be careful in how they interpret silence. Often a cause of nervousness to Anglo-Saxons, silence is regarded by the Finns in particular as a natural part of the flow of good communication. Interrupting another speaker in mid-sentence is considered impolite. If a business contact sits silently through a discussion it does not necessarily mean either that he or she is in tacit agreement with what is being said, or that negative opinions are being withheld out of courtesy. Take care not to interpret silence as disrespect. In order to be sure about the opinion someone holds ask direct questions.

Thirdly, the habit of playing the Devil's Advocate, or arguing a point even when it is not one you agree with personally, can be misunderstood by Scandinavians. Arguing in favour of a case that you manifestly do not agree with can lead to your integrity as a potential business contact being questioned.

Fourthly, most Scandinavians learn English from a young age and meetings, negotiations, correspondence and telephone calls can usually be conducted in English without difficulty. However, in general Scandinavians are proud of their language skills and may not admit when they do not understand. Basic good cross-cultural communication skills such as clarifying, checking understanding and rephrasing using different words will usually overcome any serious problems.

Finally there are some national variations across Scandinavia that should be kept in mind. Danes can come across as a little blunter than others. Norwegians have a reputation for being more informal than others while Swedes are somewhat more formal. As mentioned earlier, Finns are known for talking less than most other peoples in Europe. Scandinavian countries also have a complex history of (relatively) good-natured rivalries. These can be somewhat difficult to decipher for outsiders and are subjects best avoided in conversation.

The trend in Denmark, Norway and Sweden is to use first names in business communication once initial contact has been established. However some sectors are more formal than others and if in doubt it makes sense to stick to using a title and surname until it is obvious you can do otherwise. In Finland the use of first names requires a closer relationship and needs to be mutually agreed on. Moving from surnames to first names is generally proposed by the older or more senior party, or by women.

While English is widely spoken making an effort to greet colleagues in a local language will be appreciated. Handshakes are standard for both men and women on arrival and departure; however Scandinavia is not a touching culture and embraces or hugs in the business environment can cause embarrassment. Equally, business visitors who receive less eye contact than they are used to should take care not to misinterpret this as lack of interest. Business dress is fairly conservative, which means a business suit, shirt and tie for men and modestly cut business suits for women.

Persuading and influencing

Communicating clearly, keeping promises and following up on commitments are vitally important in developing influence with Scandinavian business contacts. While Scandinavian business is not particularly risk averse, the need for consensus in decision-making can be reflected in a low level of individual risk-taking. Generally speaking, high quality environmentally friendly products, proven and tested in practice, are likely to have a broader appeal than obviously untested and novel business solutions. Even when the business contact with whom you are negotiating is convinced of your argument, he may need to gain internal agreement to any decision to actually do business with you. The process of building an internal consensus can take time and pressing for an immediate decision can sometimes backfire. Once a decision is made the implementation is generally quick and efficient as the people who matter will already have been consulted.

The most persuasive business presentations tend to be factual and straightforward, with an emphasis on using hard data and factual information to create a convincing case. The hard sell or presentations that appeal to emotional responses are unlikely to be successful. Pointing out weaknesses or disadvantages with a particular course of action can come across as honest and will help build trust. But avoid criticising for the sake of it or playing Devil's Advocate. Modesty is important, so avoid boasting or exaggerating claims. When faced with blunt criticism of proposals the best response is to listen patiently without interrupting, demonstrate receptiveness and to respond in a positive tone.

Arrive at meetings on time and well prepared. Agendas tend to be followed fairly closely and meetings will usually start and end on time. Obviously aggressive or emotional negotiating tactics are probably best avoided, as is an overtly tactical approach to negotiation strategy or bargaining techniques. Present a firm, well researched, realistic and competitive opening offer backed up by relevant facts and figures and without overblown claims. Be prepared to argue your case in supporting your opening offer, as rapid and unanticipated changes to proposals can come across as inadequate preparation or as an obvious bargaining strategy. Although Scandinavia is not a face-oriented region, direct confrontation and frontal attacks on negotiating positions are rare. Conflicts should be approached in a positive, low key and tactful fashion with the clear aim of reaching a mutually beneficial agreement. Given the need for extended internal consensus seeking it can prove difficult to renegotiate terms after an agreement has been made, even in changed circumstances. Keeping to agreed deadlines and schedules is essential.

Dealing with hierarchies

Across Scandinavia business hierarchies tend to be flat, with flexible and team-oriented management structures. Intermediaries are rarely important in gaining access to senior levels and employees will generally feel free to cut across reporting lines wherever necessary. The boss is, at least in theory, considered a team leader rather than a key decision-maker, and relationships between corporate levels aspire towards openness and tolerance.

This is not to say that Scandinavian leaders will not be directive where necessary. The outward value attached to equality and consensus should not be confused with a complete absence of hierarchies in personal and professional relationships. Scandinavians are well aware of who is the boss and not knowing your station or over-familiarity is likely to be as unwelcome there as anywhere else. However the general aspiration is that where possible problems should be solved through negotiation and consensus, rather than pulling rank. Leaders will normally take some convincing not to endorse the recommendations of project groups or lower managers, and the best way of influencing a Scandinavian leader may well be influencing the team below him or her.

Managing people

While there are few particular surprises in managing Scandinavian colleagues, there are some general rules of thumb that will help smooth the way to effective performance. Soft skills are important in the Scandinavian management environment and the development of team cohesion and consensus is a highly valued management function.

Team meetings are usually forums for expressing and listening to opinions and it is important to ensure that time is available for all viewpoints to be heard. Individuals can be reluctant to contradict colleagues or bosses in public and it may be necessary to ask fairly specific questions in order to get a clear understanding of what people are thinking.

It has been suggested that Scandinavian workers may respond better to reward structures based on equality and egalitarianism rather than just individual performance. It is generally the case that positive feedback tends to be fairly matter of fact. Giving praise that appears over-generous or focuses on an individual rather than the team, particularly in public, may well invite suspicion rather than satisfaction.

Managing time, schedules, deadlines and bureaucracy

There are few particular challenges in dealing with time issues in Scandinavia and managing Scandinavian bureaucracy is relatively less problematic for business people than in some other European regions. Punctuality is important in both business and social situations. Appointments need to be arranged well in advance avoiding the summer months of July and August, and late December. The Scandinavian working day starts and ends relatively early.

10. The Netherlands

Despite being one of the most liberal countries on earth, Dutch culture relies on the fact that people stick to the rules and do what is expected of them. Dutch business culture both reflects and reinforces these core social attitudes.

Introduction

Internationally-minded, egalitarian and entrepreneurial, the Dutch are renowned for their open-mindedness and tolerance, values which reflect a genuine desire for co-existence and cooperation between the diverse regional, religious and social components that make up The Netherlands. Far less obvious to outsiders perhaps is the value the Dutch place on social order and conformism. In order for Dutch compromise and tolerance to work there has to be a certain respect for the laws of the land, however few of them there are.

All of these Dutch characteristics rely on a shared desire for consensus and an occasionally conservative attitude towards change. Customers and business contacts are certainly respected, but giving the impression of superiority or making unreasonable or unfair demands is unlikely to be tolerated. Company communication lines are clear and direct and workplace relationships are marked by an egalitarian approach in which discussion and consensus-seeking are key elements of good work practice.

The cultural background to business in The Netherlands

Tolerance, consensus and compromise

It was not until the 16th Century that the part of northern Europe which now includes most of the Netherlands, Belgium and Luxembourg became a distinct political entity. The original Dutch uprising against Spanish colonial rule resulted in the Republic of the Netherlands, comprised of semi-independent duchies and provinces. In order to achieve anything in this Republic it was necessary for the various components that made up Dutch society to form coalitions of one sort or another. As the nation developed, four distinct social coalitions appeared. Each of these coalitions, Catholic, Protestant, Socialist and Liberal, had its own schools, newspapers, industries and neighbourhoods. Individuals relied to a significant extent on their membership of these columns for identity and social support. Working effectively within coalitions then, as now, demanded consensus around goals and detailed planning. The ability to avoid causing unnecessary alienation of opponents and to avoid standing out too much from mainstream opinion came to be seen as basic survival skills. Success came through tolerance, the demonstration of respect for others, and a willingness to listen and compromise.

Today much of the Dutch cultural model is still based on a collectivistic desire not to impose one's point of view on others. The Dutch saying *'Doe maar gewoon, dan doe je al gek genoeg'* (rough translation: 'Just act normal, it's strange enough') neatly describes the cultural value attached to keeping one's head down, not standing out from the crowd, and not overdoing things. The freedom to live life in an unconventional or sometimes even bizarre way, which is the stereotypical European image of the Netherlands, depends on the condition that individuals accept the pressure of social control and ultimately behave normally, particularly when it comes to showing tolerance and respect for others. It also has to be said that much of the Netherland's social liberalism is marked as much by indifference to what others get up to as it is by real tolerance.

As elsewhere in Europe the demands placed on the Dutch cultural model by large scale immigration and the resulting ethnic and religious mix have led to significant rethink on how society should work. Nevertheless, the desire for consensus and compromise is to some extent hard-wired into the Dutch psyche and nowhere is this more apparent than in the business environment. Decision-making in Dutch organisations is guided by the need to reach and maintain consensus to a greater extent than in almost any other European country. For example, every company employing more than 35 people is required by law to have an *ondernemingsraad*, or workers' council, that has to be consulted on all major policy issues.

Calvinism and conformity

Calvinism was a particularly strict version of Protestant Christian faith that hugely influenced the development of Dutch culture from the 16th Century onwards. The religion emphasises that all people are born equal but imperfect and are prone to sin. An individual's task on earth is to scrutinise his or her own behaviour for signs of sin, and eradicate them as much as possible. As a practicing religion Calvinism has limited influence in the modern-day Netherlands, in fact one of Europe's most secular nations. All the same its vestiges are apparent in Dutch culture in such values as an attachment to soul-searching, self-criticism and egalitarianism. The strong Dutch work ethic, moderation, a belief in orderliness, and a desire not to appear boastful but rather to *just act normal* can all be traced to the influence of Calvinism. The Dutch education system continues to reinforce these values. Children are taught to be assertive and make their own choices but also to co-operate and compromise with others.

In the Dutch work environment one influence of Calvinism is the strong attachment to honesty, clarity and straightforwardness as an essential element of effective professional communication. For overseas business visitors, particularly those from Anglo-Saxon cultures, this communication style can sometimes come across as overly direct or even blunt. In business discussions the Dutch can be significantly more inclined to express direct criticism, whether of themselves or others, than is the case elsewhere. It is best for business visitors to view this critical approach as a sign of interest and involvement in the issues at hand, rather than any desire to be discourteous. Criticism that appears blunt or even rude is usually designed to be helpful.

Overleg and Beleid

The Dutch word *Overleg*, roughly translated as deliberation, describes an occasionally lengthy process by which groups work towards reaching a compromise decision, whether in business or elsewhere. *Overleg* strongly influences the way in which information is exchanged and discussions take place. The word *Beleid* describes the stated policy or aims of a company or organisation and the activities the organisation undertakes to achieve policy goals. *Beleid* comes into being through the process of *Overleg* and serves to make business processes and goals explicit and unambiguous for everyone in the company. Every individual within the company has to act within the agreed *Beleid*. At its best the behaviours associated with *Overleg* and *Beleid* carry the implication that everyone should be listened to, and that the end result of discussion should be shared consensus. At its worst *Overleg* has been associated with a meeting culture unrivalled anywhere else in Europe, in which long and sometimes fierce debate is too easily seen as a method for regulating process, or a solution in itself, rather than a means to an end.

Building relationships

Establishing close personal relationships with Dutch business contacts is not as important as in other parts of Europe. Instead the focus tends to be on dealing professionally with the issues at hand in a clear and transparent manner. That said, the Dutch value a personal approach and business socialising is not uncommon. Lunches, and to a lesser extent dinners, take place on a regular basis and serve as forums for continuing business discussions. Social events tend to be scheduled and planned in advance and it may be difficult for business contacts to respond positively to last minute invitations.

The most successful social occasions tend to be those that fit in with the Dutch and Belgian concept of *gezelligheid*. Roughly translatable as cosy or pleasant, *gezelligheid* implies that the best social occasions are low-key, with the main focus on a comfortable mood, good food and drink and the enjoyment of good company. Choosing to entertain business contacts in obviously expensive and ostentatious restaurants carries the risk of appearing immodest, or even boastful. Carefully selecting an attractive *gezelligheid* location with an obviously relaxing and even subdued atmosphere will reduce this risk. Most restaurants include gratuities in the bill and tipping ostentatiously is also likely to be viewed as immodest.

Flowers, chocolates, houseplants or thoughtfully selected wine are all acceptable gifts if you are invited for dinner at a Dutch home. Otherwise gift-giving does not form an important part of Dutch business culture. If you do wish to give a gift, it is probably sensible to do so to celebrate a successful contract rather than at the outset of any relationship. The best gifts are carefully selected but manifestly modest. Expensive gifts can cause embarrassment and may be interpreted as inappropriate.

Business cards are commonly exchanged. As a high-level of competence in English is widespread through the Netherlands it is not necessary to have business cards translated. Promotional materials, manuals and standard contracts should be translated into Dutch wherever possible, particularly when dealing with complex or unusual terms.

Making the right impression

Dutch communication styles tend to be direct, clear and unambiguous, and the ability to read between the lines may not be as well developed as elsewhere. As a consequence business people from countries with a less direct style, such as the UK, may need to be more explicit when communicating, particularly when giving feedback or constructive criticism. It is also important not to misinterpret forcefully expressed ideas as discourteous or confrontational. Instead, the Dutch tendency to ask challenging questions in a direct manner can productively be seen in two ways: firstly as an integral underpinning of their willingness to innovate or experiment in business, and secondly as a way of avoiding unwelcome secrets in the work environment. Dutch companies are renowned for giving out more information to staff and customers than would be considered appropriate elsewhere. Any hesitance in answering questions in a clear and straightforward way can be seen by Dutch business contacts as unwillingness to share relevant information.

Business interactions tend, at least initially, to be somewhat more formal than those in Anglo-Saxon cultures. When addressing unfamiliar business contacts it is probably sensible to use titles (Mr or *Mijnheer* for a man, Mrs, Ms or *Mevrouw* for a woman) followed by a last name, until it is clear you can use first names. Older people or those outside the more cosmopolitan and urban parts of the country may take longer to feel comfortable with the use of first names. Professional titles such as lawyer, doctor or engineer are hardly ever used when speaking although are commonly used in business correspondence. Business letters can usually be written in English and should maintain a formal tone, even if you are on first name terms with the recipient.

Unsurprisingly in such an open culture there are few taboo subjects in conversations with Dutch contacts. Religion is seen as a private issue and is probably best avoided. Otherwise, robust discussion is welcome on most subjects including recent political events.

Greetings are similar to those encountered elsewhere in Western Europe. Handshakes are common at the beginning and end of meetings and between men and women. Maintaining good eye-contact is important, although strong smiles are not common in business in formal business settings and tend to be reserved for close family and friends.

Business dress in the Netherlands tends to be fairly conservative, although this depends to a certain extent on the business sector and age of counterparts. In the more traditional sectors men wear dark suits with shirts and ties, while women wear suits or skirts and white blouses. Many successful Dutch entrepreneurs, particularly in newer business sectors, make significant efforts to dress down.

Wearing obviously expensive labels in any work environment can come across as ostentatious and possibly even pretentious. When in doubt about appropriate dress it makes sense to ask local colleagues and remain on the conservative side.

Persuading and influencing

In a country as task-focused as the Netherlands hard facts, figures and empirical data will always be more persuasive than personal intuition or unsupported supposition.

However, the tone in which data is presented can be of vital importance in maximising the persuasiveness of your business arguments. In particular business people should take care not to present information in a way that comes across as overstated, inflated or conceited. The best sales presentations are simple, factual and understated, and let the data speak. Supporting documentation needs to be clear and concise and written in simple low-key language. Words that even hint at showing off or boasting about company achievements, product superiority or individual expertise can create the wrong impression, even if what is being said is fundamentally true.

Generally speaking the Dutch will rarely spend a lot of time socialising before a negotiation or meeting. Once the necessary introductions are made they will tend to move directly to the business at hand. In negotiations it is important to avoid over-promising or ambiguity in responding to specific requests. Tentative answers such as 'we'll see', 'it might be possible' or 'perhaps', sound evasive and lack clarity from a Dutch point of view. Saying no when you mean no is likely to come across to Dutch contacts as more honest and straightforward, and ultimately more beneficial for long-term business relationships.

Promises need to be kept, no matter how casual or inconsequential they may appear. Changing or revisiting an agreement after it has been confirmed is unlikely to endear you to your contacts.

Business visitors from cultures that value quick decision-making may also need to think carefully about how speedily they can conclude negotiations in the Netherlands. The importance attached to consensus in companies means that decisions may take longer to emerge than elsewhere. This can be frustrating on occasion but it is sensible for visitors to focus on the positive benefits of this process. Most of the key people will already have been consulted before a decision is finalised, which at least in theory removes the need to sell a decision to a potentially sceptical team. Follow through also tends to be quicker once a deal is established, as many of the key planning details have already been settled and commitments agreed as part of the decision-making process.

Dealing with hierarchies

Given the egalitarian nature of society in general, it is unsurprising that there is a fairly functional attitude to hierarchical differences in the Dutch business environment. In theory at least, everyone in a company from the top manager to the most junior employee is considered valuable and worthy of respect in his or her own right. Hierarchies exist in order to manage complex organisations, but there is no particular status attached to seniority, or around age, gender, educational qualification, or much else. As a result strictly enforced corporate hierarchies with overly directive managers can make Dutch employees uncomfortable. In contrast, individuals at every organisational level are encouraged to contribute to decision-making by making their opinions known. Expressing considered opinions in a clear way is significantly more important in the work environment than attempting to please superiors.

Foreign businesswomen should encounter few problems in working in the Netherlands. It is common to find women at all levels in the Dutch business environment although the fact that many have part-time jobs can sometimes limit their chances for upward mobility.

Managing people

There are several areas in which business visitors to the Netherlands may need to review their management styles when dealing with Dutch staff.

Firstly, in a culture in which value is attached to straightforward plain-speaking and constructive criticism, it might be expected managers would give fairly direct feedback to employees on their performance. In fact, negative feedback to subordinates in the work environment is often delivered in a careful and guarded way. In this particular instance the Dutch belief in egalitarianism means that emphasis is laid on avoiding workplace confrontation. From the Dutch perspective the best way to manage and motivate subordinates can often be to give them clearly defined objectives with a high degree of personal discretion. Criticising individuals for using this discretion makes little sense. When problems occur, blame is often apportioned to the system or unanticipated events rather than to any one individual. Constructive criticism is directed squarely at the system, and sometimes only obliquely at the individuals involved.

Giving positive feedback can also sometimes be problematic. As a significant amount of work is approached though the process of *Overleg* (group deliberation), open competition between workers is sometimes frowned upon. Feedback that recognises and rewards individual effort needs also to take explicit account of the group context in which the work is performed. Whether positive or negative, feedback is best delivered in private and may well be questioned by the recipient.

Secondly, anticipate considerable resistance to decisions perceived as being imposed from outside without consultation, particularly in areas considered to be in shared spheres of influence. There is a clear need to be sensitive to the Dutch belief in egalitarian decision-making. In practical terms this may mean making efforts to be open to suggestions from all levels in the organisation, and being more open with information than normal. It also means making the effort to find out as much as possible about the particular decision-making processes in any company you are involved with. Do not forget to enquire about the status of the company council, which can sometimes be an influential participant in decision-making.

Thirdly, avoid probing too keenly into the details of a colleague's family or private life. The Dutch belief in tolerance and individual freedom means that family and business lives are often kept distinct. Details of one's private life are rarely discussed in the work environment.

Finally, take care when requesting rapid or unanticipated changes in direction from colleagues. Spontaneity is not a key value in Dutch business culture and there may be resistance to changes in direction that have not been fully discussed or understood. Showing impatience or insisting that changes are made as quickly as possible may well invite resistance, as it can indicate to Dutch colleagues that the original planning process was faulty.

Managing time, schedules, deadlines and bureaucracy

Planning, managing, and organising are key values in Dutch culture and significant value is attached to the efficient and productive use of time. Punctuality is essential for both business and social engagements. Appointments are carefully scheduled and there may be considerable resistance to last minute changes to appointments, schedules or deadlines.

Office hours are generally 8.30 am to 5.30 pm, although senior staff will work longer. Appointments can be difficult to arrange during the summer holiday period in July and August, and over the Christmas period in late December.

11. Poland

Poland is often regarded by outsiders as a typical Eastern European country. In fact this is a relatively recent perception. Historically, the Polish people have seen their own nation as belonging squarely in central Europe at the boundary between East and West.

Introduction

Despite centuries of foreign incursions into Polish territory, including repeated invasion, dismemberment and incorporation into other states, the Polish cultural identity can be traced back over 1,000 years. This uninterrupted and powerful sense of nationhood, dictated to a great extent by geography, religion and history, continues to have a number of identifiable influences on Polish business culture. Understanding these influences and what they mean for business etiquette, structures and practices will help international business visitors to perform effectively in the Polish business environment.

The cultural background to business in Poland

History and identity

Poland has been constantly influenced by its neighbours to the East and the West, and control of its political and economic security has alternated between these powerful and often aggressive influences. During the period of Soviet domination Poland enjoyed relatively greater freedom than other countries in the Eastern Bloc. Nevertheless there continues to be reluctance in accepting cultural influences or political pressure from Russia. In a similar vein the nation's persistently strained relationships with Germany can best be understood in the light of its experiences before and during the Second World War.

In place of local cultural influences Poland has historically looked to countries further afield. Connections with Western Europe date back to the year 966 when Poland's acceptance of Christianity led to independent statehood. More recently, massive Polish emigration to the USA led to a range of American influences on lifestyles and business, as well as that nation becoming a source of political support and legitimacy. The current Polish constitution and modern attitudes towards political and constitutional freedoms find many of their roots in North American and Anglo-Saxon social structures.

This is not to say that Western influences have been accepted uncritically in Poland. Polish writers have written of the 'headache of freedom' involved in Poland's recent adjustment to democratic government. Poles have always had mixed feelings about influences from the West, perhaps because the West has continuously failed to meet expectations. Nevertheless business people from the United States, particularly those working in areas such as financial services, can sometimes be regarded by some Poles as better educated, or better specialists, or people to learn from. They are likely to be respected in advance in a way that people from other areas would not be.

Modern Polish business culture is heavily influenced by North American styles of management even if there is a discrepancy between the idealised American way of doing business and the practical Polish side of doing business. Many young Poles, particularly those who have chosen to join global companies, are likely to have made a conscious choice to work in what they perceive to be a western way. This has lead to behaviours that on occasion fit uncomfortably within more traditional Polish approaches to work.

Hierarchy and conflict

Polish society reacted to extended periods of foreign domination by developing a form of mental resistance to those perceived as imposing alien traditions or of limiting freedom. Historically it was seen as almost improper to work hard for foreign governments or systems. Although Polish business culture is marked by a relatively strong respect for hierarchy and authority, there may be a parallel tendency to resist decisions obviously imposed from outside without consultation. This can make life difficult for foreign managers in Poland as feedback from subordinates to bosses can be much less direct than in Anglo-Saxon cultures. Polish employees may be unwilling to demonstrate opposition to senior staff, even when they know that something is not going right. The result is that turnover of subordinates can be very high where foreign managers are unable to read between the lines in conversation. Bosses who are more sincere and relationship-focused tend to receive the best feedback.

Religion and family

During the extended periods in history when Poland did not exist as a country the Polish church was one of the few institutions to uphold and maintain the Polish sense of nationhood. Even during the most difficult period of oppression in the 1950s, the Roman Catholic Church never became fully subservient to the communist regime.

The vast majority of the Polish population still describe themselves as Catholic and the interconnected relationship between Church and nation provides the Polish people with a strong sense of continuity, shared belief and solidarity. Polish social traditions including attitudes towards divorce, sexuality, family and relationships continue to be linked to a conservative form of Catholicism to an extent that can surprise foreigners. Polish critics of the Roman Catholic Church's influence, of whom there are many, sometimes condemn the way religion is expressed in Poland as nationalistic and anti-modern. Whether that is true or not, it is certainly the case that Poland remains one of the most socially conservative nations in Europe in which traditional family life is valued above most other things.

Paradoxically perhaps this social conservatism does not extend to an absence of women in the workplace. Women are present in the public sphere in large numbers, and a significant proportion of the working population is female, with women particularly well represented in the legal and medical professions.

Building relationships

To a greater extent than in some other European cultures, hospitality is something that takes place at home. Business visitors may well be invited to private homes to socialise more often than elsewhere. Gifts such as wine, flowers or house plants are appropriate when visiting a private home. Gift-giving, apart from small gifts at first meetings, is otherwise not a part of Polish business culture.

Business lunches and dinners usually start earlier than elsewhere; around noon or 1pm for lunch, and as early as 6pm for dinner. Meals are social occasions so if it is necessary to bring up the subject of business wait until your business partner does so or at least give an advance warning that you need to discuss some business issues. Tip around 10% in restaurants.

When socialising alcohol, particularly vodka, will be consumed on a regular basis. It is perfectly acceptable to decline alcoholic drinks or ask for mixers. Avoid drinking until the host has proposed a toast. The first toast is usually raised by the host to the guests and you should reciprocate by standing and drinking to the health of the hosts. The Polish phrase *na zdrowie* has the equivalent function of 'Cheers' in English.

Making the right impression

Until the 1990s Russian was a compulsory language in primary and secondary schools and many older Poles retain a working knowledge of the language. Many of those holding senior positions in today's business world are relatively young and are less likely to know Russian. In recent years English and German have become the most practiced foreign languages amongst this younger cadre, partly as a result of the widespread development of private language schools and, in the case of English, the influence of the estimated 750,000 Poles who have lived and worked in the UK for a period of time. It may still be the case however that Polish business contacts have limited competence in other languages, so visitors should try to check the language skills of potential contacts in advance.

Polish is certainly one of the most difficult European languages to learn with grammatical forms rarely encountered elsewhere and a particularly rich lexis of proverbs and sayings. Polish uses the Latin alphabet but without the letters Q, V and X, except in foreign words. Despite the difficulty in learning Polish, business visitors would benefit from using some basic phrases to show courtesy and willingness to engage with local business contacts. Useful phrases include *dzien dobry* for 'hello', *do widzenia* for 'goodbye', and *dziekuje* for 'thank you'.

Polish names are arranged in the same way as in Anglo-Saxon countries, with the first name followed by a single surname. The use of first names in business is becoming more common, particularly amongst younger Polish people. Nevertheless, if in doubt it is sensible to mirror your host's behaviour, and initially to stick to titles like *Pan* or Mr, *Pani* or Mrs, and *Panno* or Ms, followed by your contact's surname until it is obvious first names are acceptable. Professional titles such as Doctor or Engineer are rarely used in the Polish business world.

There are few surprises in the area of non-verbal communication in Poland. Business contacts are perhaps likely to smile less than in other countries. This is rarely a reflection of unfriendliness; smiles tend to be reserved for family members and close acquaintances rather than business contacts. Showing a fixed smile to strangers can be confusing for Polish contacts. Good eye contact is important during conversation and handshaking is appropriate with both men and women of all ages.

The traditional male custom of kissing a woman's hand on meeting may occasionally still be seen but is certainly not something business visitors need to copy. It is important however for visitors to bear in mind that male courtesies towards women, such as letting women pass through the door first, offering seats to women on public transport, or offering to carry heavy bags, are not seen as anachronistic or sexist. Equality in the Polish work environment is seen as perfectly compatible with traditional femininity. Mannered courtesy and formality towards Polish women demonstrates respect and should be understood in that way.

Business cards are used frequently and should be exchanged whenever meeting new contacts. You might consider having one side of your business cards printed in Polish.

There are few taboos in conversation with Polish contacts. Jokes about religion should certainly be avoided but otherwise humour is welcome in social situations, although less so in the business environment. Demonstrating obvious ignorance about Polish history or the nation's significant achievements in science, literature and art is unlikely to gain many friends.

Business dress is similar to elsewhere in central Europe. In larger or more traditional companies dark suits and ties are usual. In smaller or medium-sized companies casual clothes are more common. On business visits it makes sense to dress formally unless you are certain that a more casual style is acceptable.

Persuading and influencing

Take care also not to assume that Polish contacts are inevitably task-driven. Good relationships are important in Polish business culture and there is a general preference for doing initial business face-to-face. Behaviour that comes across as stubborn, inflexible or unpredictable may indicate that the required level of personal trust has not been established.

First meetings are likely to be fairly formal and are aimed at sizing up potential partners. Decisions are unlikely to be made unless the decision makers are present at a negotiation or meeting, and it may take several meetings before any final decisions are reached. In general it makes sense to anticipate a slower overall process of decision-making than in Anglo-Saxon cultures. When entering a meeting or negotiation wait for the host to point you to an appropriate seat. Greeting everyone in the room is important, preferably after a third-party introduction. Small talk is likely to be less extended than elsewhere and making jokes at initial stages can be misunderstood.

Executives or negotiating teams should ideally be of a similar status to those in the Polish business you are dealing with. Once negotiations have started Polish negotiators can appear reserved. Periods of silence during negotiations are best seen as part of formal communication rather than an absence of communication. Do not try to fill the silence with unnecessary talk even if you feel uncomfortable.

The most influential presentations tend to be heavy on data, tailored to the specific interests of the company you are dealing with and supported by relevant statistics and case studies. It is also important to provide sufficient information about your company and background as it is on this basis that initial trust is built.

Dealing with hierarchies

Hierarchies and status are important in Polish business culture although not necessarily in the same way as elsewhere. Seniority in age, title and position, and educational background are important and particular attention and respect should be paid both to older members of the company and to those in senior roles. However, stereotypically feminine traits are often valued more highly than stereotypically masculine traits, and women are present at all levels of the Polish workforce. Emotionality and sensitivity in interpersonal relations is important regardless of one's sex, and many Polish people tend to place importance on the building and maintaining of close personal relationships in order to get things done. It is often the case that outsiders need to make particular efforts to earn the trust of people at senior levels in the Polish business hierarchy before a close relationship forms. Thankfully for overseas business visitors the Poles are renowned for their hospitality and socialising is a fairly important element of building business relationships.

Managing people

A key element in managing Polish colleagues effectively is a good understanding of and adaptability to local communication styles. Managers need to listen carefully as opposition by subordinates may only be hinted at. However, when communicating with people at the same hierarchical level or even with distant business contacts, Polish opinions can be expressed forcefully. Debate is often robust and occasionally confrontational. To those unfamiliar with Polish communication styles, discussion may appear to be very fierce. Frank expression, even sometimes at the expense of being hurtful to someone, has been described as a core value within Polish communication. Westerners in particular can feel lost, sometimes even offended by the strength of the gestures and remarks being made. As a well known Polish saying has it, three political parties emerge when two Poles have a discussion.

Business visitors to Poland also need to be aware that Polish native speakers sometimes use different intonation patterns to English speakers. On occasion when these Polish language intonation patterns are transferred to English they can falsely carry a disinterested or discourteous tone to native speakers of English. It is equally important for overseas managers not to mistake the tone of Polish conversation. The imperative form (i.e. give me the information) is usually used in English for giving direct orders, and can sound inappropriately abrupt in business situations. Polish does not have any supposed relationship between politeness and the use of the imperative and foreign managers should not assume that direct requests are meant to be impolite. In general it makes sense to avoid assuming that direct, blunt communication is designed to be confrontational. It is more often designed to be helpful.

Basic communication good practice is likely to ensure effective interaction with Polish colleagues. Keep sentences in English short and simple and make space for everyone to participate in meetings. If you are not receiving the kind of feedback then make it clear that it is acceptable for Polish colleagues to give constructive feedback in these circumstances, or change the context. For example, ask individuals privately for comments or raise the subject in a social situation. Avoid using nuance, hidden meanings or complicated humour when you speak and do not be afraid to repeat yourself. If in doubt, question and clarify, repeating back what you think you have heard in your own words and ask for confirmation. Finally, in Polish teams do not think trust will just happen. It needs working on.

Managing times, schedules, deadlines and bureaucracy

Inefficiencies and delays in the legal system, inflexible employment laws (despite relatively high unemployment), persistent bureaucratic residues of the Soviet era, and continuing corruption will all impact on business in Poland. Business visitors will encounter red tape in many areas and Polish bureaucracy can be as challenging to deal with as any in Europe. It makes sense to anticipate that even relatively simple business deals may involve more paperwork than elsewhere. Having a Polish business partner who understands regulations and can track changes in the law will help. As with much of Polish business, being patient, polite and courteous and establishing good personal relationships will help smooth business red tape. On occasion foreigners can expect and demand slightly faster service, although this cannot be relied on.

Office hours are earlier than elsewhere in Europe, often from around 8am to 4pm, or longer for more senior staff. Appointments are best scheduled for mid-morning or early to mid-afternoon.

It is sensible to anticipate a need for flexibility in scheduling appointments on the part of Polish contacts, and appointment times can change at short notice. Nevertheless, once a time is agreed punctuality is important and meetings or calls are expected to start and usually finish on time. For social situations it is sensible to arrive between 15 and 30 minutes after the scheduled time.

12. Hungary

A unique language, forty years of relative isolation during the communist period, a complex ethnic identity, and an eventful history have lead many in Hungary to question the extent to which the country can be considered as part of mainstream European culture.

Introduction

Whether Hungary is part of central and Eastern Europe or is culturally quite distinct is a debate pursued by, and probably best left to, Hungarians. It is perhaps sufficient for foreign business people to remember that while much of Hungarian business culture and etiquette is broadly similar to what they can find elsewhere in Europe, there are also cultural traits that make aspects of doing business in Hungary highly distinctive. These range from Hungary's complex and idiosyncratic language, through to a cultural affinity for strong family relationships and mutual responsibility, to what has been defined as Hungarian 'pessimism'. These and other characteristics impact on the behaviour and expectations of Hungarian business people. Of course, Hungarians are all individuals, and the country has traditionally maintained a strong division between urban and rural ways of doing things. Nevertheless, finding out more about these distinctive Hungarian characteristics, and the rules of thumb for dealing with them, is likely to smooth the way to effective business in Hungary.

The cultural background to business in Hungary

Language and communication styles

Unrelated to any of the languages spoken in neighbouring countries, the closest relatives to the Hungarian language can be found in distant Estonia and Finland. As elsewhere, language plays a major part in Hungary's national and regional cultural identity and is a source of much national pride.

The use of the Hungarian language is characterised by some distinct communication styles that Hungarians often carry with them when communicating in other languages. Firstly, the language is highly descriptive. Verbal dexterity, a rich and occasionally even exaggerated use of language, and the ability to debate vigorously are all highly prized. Consequently, what can appear to business visitors to be heated or emotional discussion may not in reality imply hostility or antagonism, but instead simply reflect a desire to use language in an attractive and fluent manner. It is important for visitors not to mistake intense but controlled debate for something more serious. An occasional loss of control in expressing emotions is at the least readily forgiven, and is often preferred to bland pleasantries or evasiveness.

Secondly, Hungarian culture attaches value to a fairly direct and explicit communication style. Viewpoints tend to be expressed with absolute clarity and robustness. Business visitors who fail to demonstrate sufficient clarity in their own language can sometimes raise suspicions that they are not to be trusted or have something to hide. This affinity for clarity and directness in communication is associated with a common Hungarian belief that criticism is best seen as a form of social responsibility, and only those for whom criticism is justified will be offended by it. From the Hungarian perspective, people are often directly responsible for their own misfortune. To quote a Hungarian proverb: *'If it is not your shirt, don't wear it'.*

Thirdly, Hungarian possesses a highly complex system for expressing different levels of politeness depending on who is taking part in a conversation. Being polite in day-to-day dealings, treating counterparts with thoughtfulness and courtesy, and using proper etiquette all contribute to demonstrating and earning respect. Formality, hospitality, politeness and good manners are important not just in terms of language. Although the younger generation of Hungarians tends to be more casual, Hungarian men are still expected to be 'gentlemen', offering their seats to women, opening doors and paying the bill in restaurants.

Family

Hungarians, particularly in rural areas, have traditionally maintained close bonds beyond the immediate family towards a wider network of extended family. Members of this extended network are expected to provide mutual support when required. In the countryside, for example, extended families may join together to help one of their number to build a new home.

In the business environment while the development of long-standing personal relationships is not as much of a key driver in Hungarian business as in southern Europe, it is still the case that building mutual trust and developing effective networks is an important part of effective business. Who you know can be an important indicator of your trustworthiness, and on occasion the high level of commitment to family and friends can extend to excluding those who are seen as outsiders. In the initial stages of a business relationship Hungarians may sometimes appear reserved and suspicious, and it may take a while for sufficient trust to be established to undertake business.

Hungarian 'pessimism'

Hungary is a cultured and sophisticated country whose people demonstrate a strong sense of national and ethnic pride. Paradoxically perhaps, Hungarians are also inclined to a certain level of pessimism with regard to their own lives and their country's position in the world. Some social scientists have even speculated that Hungarians have a genetic predisposition to suicide, sometimes described as the *"Melancholy Magyar"* theory. This inclination has been aggravated by chronic defeatism following a history of lost wars and a feeling of hopelessness during the communist era. Whether or not one accepts the notion of a genetic predisposition, it is certainly true that Hungary's statistical incidence of mental disorders and depression is extremely high. The country also has one of the world's highest suicide rates; approximately three times that of the United States or the UK.

A somewhat paradoxical impact of pessimism can be seen in the fact that Hungarians can be extremely ambitious at work. Indeed, up until very recently leisure time was not perceived as a high priority issue even for the younger generations. While things have changed significantly in recent times, high levels of family and social expectation still mean that the leisure time of many Hungarians, both young and old, is likely to be channelled towards further personal or professional achievement, rather than the leisure pursuits common in western European cultures.

'Face' and status consciousness

Status, and in particular the position that results from age and education, is a further important element in the Hungarian cultural make-up. It is important for Hungarians to be offered the appropriate level of *face* associated with their position in the social hierarchy. The value attached to *face* is reflected in the Hungarian language, in which special grammatical structures are used to express particular respect to older people, strangers, or those higher in the hierarchy. In business situations foreign visitors would do well to make every effort to find out the relative status of their business contacts, and avoid causing counterparts to lose face. Putting Hungarian business contacts in situations that threaten their dignity or self-respect is the quickest way to lose influence.

Building relationships

Establishing mutual trust is an important aspect of building productive relationships with Hungarian business contacts and, as elsewhere, giving and receiving hospitality is a key element of building this trust. Business visitors to Hungary should aim to accept as many social invitations as reasonable and reciprocate wherever possible. If you have to turn down an offer or invitation, make sure that business contacts do not lose face and that you give a credible reason for not attending.

Lunch, generally eaten between noon and 2 pm, is the most frequent business meal. Dinners are also common and tend to start at around 7 or 8pm. Meals are social occasions rather than forums for business discussions, so as a general rule it is probably best to let Hungarian contacts initiate any business discussion. If invited to a Hungarian contact's home for dinner, be on time, bring a small gift, and leave by 9.30pm unless invited to stay longer. Be sure to show your appreciation and enjoyment of whatever dishes are offered to you.

Hungary has one of the world's highest rates of alcohol consumption, and wine in particular is likely to be available at both business lunches and dinners. There is no obligation to drink alcohol if you do not wish to. Tipping at around 10% is ubiquitous in restaurants, taxis and elsewhere.

Business cards are frequently used and exchanged without any particular ritual. It can be sensible to have one side of the card translated into Hungarian although this is not essential. Include professional titles, job role and academic qualifications as these will help your contacts understand more about you and where you fit in the organisation.

Making the right impression

Luckily for foreign visitors (given the complexity of their language) many Hungarians speak a second or third language to a good level. Russian and to a lesser extent German predominate amongst older generations, while English is the language of choice among the young. As elsewhere it is helpful to find out the level of foreign language competence of business contacts. Where necessary, choose your own interpreter rather than relying on the one provided by business partners as it can cause your partners to lose face if you need to question aspects of the interpretation they have arranged. Most written marketing and legal materials will need to be translated into Hungarian.

Learning some basic phrases in Hungarian is useful in demonstrating respect for and a willingness to engage with business contacts. Personal greetings are quite brief and frequently used. Older or more senior people are greeted with the formal *Jó napot,* while younger or more familiar people are greeted with the less formal *Szia!* Verbal greetings are usually accompanied by short, firm handshakes and strong eye contact. Handshakes take place when greeting and when leaving, but are not commonly used with people who work together on a regular basis. In general older men offer handshakes to younger men while men generally wait for women to extend hands first. Some older Hungarian men may follow the custom of bowing to a woman while shaking her hand. This is designed to demonstrate respect and it makes sense to interpret the behaviour in this way. The elderly should normally be greeted first, and are sometimes addressed as *bacsi* for men or *neni* for women used after their first name. These words literally mean uncle and aunt but are not used to signify family relationships.

When making introductions in business surnames are generally given first, followed by the first name and whatever title is relevant. Use surnames and the relevant title (i.e. Mr, Mrs or Miss) unless and until your counterpart invites you to move to first name terms. Doctors and teachers have significant status and are often addressed with special terms: *Doctor ur / Doctor no* for male / female doctors, and *Tanar ur / Tanar no* for male / female teachers. The word *Tegeződjünk* is sometimes used to indicate that it is acceptable for business contacts to move from a formal to an informal relationship.

Many younger Hungarian women retain their own names after marriage. Others construct a name from their husband's surname, followed by his first name ending in *'-ne'*, followed by the woman's maiden surname followed by her first name. If unsure it is probably sensible to ask what name to use with someone to whom you have just been introduced. Also, remember that this name ordering does not apply to Western European or American names; if you are Ms Jane Doe in the USA then you are Ms Jane Doe in Hungary. Whatever names you use, make sure you learn to pronounce them correctly. If in doubt, ask.

Business dress tends to be fairly formal, with dark business suits, shirts and ties the norm for men and business suits or dresses customary for women. Social occasions outside the work environment tend to call for smart casual clothing of demonstrable quality, and should be on the smarter side when visiting the theatre, opera, or concerts.

There are few real taboos when in conversation with Hungarian business contacts. As elsewhere in Europe it is probably sensible to avoid the topic of religion in conversation. Unless you have a clear appreciation of the complexities relating to Hungary's various ethnic minorities, particularly the country's Roma gypsy minority (who face manifest prejudice and discrimination), it may also be wise to avoid discussion in this area.

Understanding non-verbal communication in Hungary is unlikely to present any particular challenges. Eye contact tends to be somewhat stronger and more direct than in some other parts of Europe. Avoiding eye contact can sometimes be interpreted as reluctance to engage, so it makes sense to mirror the level of eye contact you are receiving from Hungarian business contacts. Smiling tends to be reserved for friends or family and frequent smiling in a business meeting has the potential to cause confusion.

Persuading and influencing

As elsewhere, initial business meetings in Hungary are mainly an opportunity to size up potential business contacts and determine if there is a base on which to build trust. Wherever possible try to arrange face-to-face meetings. Agendas can often be seen as flexible springboards to further discussion rather than route maps, and small talk before and after meetings is commonplace. It is sensible to clarify any time constraints you have at the outset of meetings, and to let business contacts bring up business issues first.

Hungarians tend to take a fairly detail-oriented approach to discussions and may be uncomfortable with broad-brush agreements that leave details to be settled later on. As a consequence it may be necessary to adapt your expectations about how quickly decisions can be made or agreements reached. If you have a strict timetable for decision-making it is sensible to make this clear in advance, and prepare to address apparently minor details fully.

Traditional Hungarian negotiators are likely to be relationship-focused, with a direct, expressive and courteous approach. Conflict tends to be handled head-on, although it is important to be attentive to issues of hierarchy and status and avoid causing contacts to lose face. A certain amount of reflective silence is common before giving answers or responding to proposals. This is designed to indicate serious consideration, so avoid the temptation to fill the silence with further comments of your own. As elsewhere prolonged silence may well signify disagreement, opposition or hostility. Having stated their opinions on a subject once Hungarians will not generally see it necessary to reiterate what they have already expressed. Repetition of arguments can be seen as pushy and as wasting time. Make the effort to remain friendly and diplomatic throughout the negotiation and keep in mind that clarifying expectations on all sides is likely to help avoid misunderstandings. Demonstrating politeness and respect, and eschewing confrontational behaviour or high-pressure sales tactics, will go a long way to resolving difficulties.

Contracts should be clear, concise and unambiguous. Hungarian bureaucracy and red-tape is legendary, and litigation is notoriously slow and expensive. Wherever possible it makes sense to aim for an agreed resolution to conflicts.

Dealing with hierarchies

Hierarchy and relative status are important in Hungarian business. Status is determined by a person's profession, experience, education, work role, and to a certain extent age.

As elsewhere, emphasising personal integrity and professional competence, and demonstrating aptitude, stamina, and self-discipline, is likely to establish credibility with individuals at all levels in the hierarchy.

Managing people

As a general rule of thumb, a hands-on, pragmatic management style is likely to prove most effective in managing Hungarian colleagues. People respond best to managers they feel they can respect and trust, rather than to those they perceive as overly directive or who fail to communicate adequately. In particular Hungarians expect to be listened to by those in senior positions and are unlikely to carry out instructions effectively without understanding the rationale, no matter the position of the person giving an order. Effective managers sustain respect through 'rolling up their sleeves'; working alongside subordinates; continuously demonstrating professionalism; being decisive but not dogmatic; and demonstrating a willingness to listen. Expressing controlled emotion, provided it is not directed at a particular individual, is also usually acceptable.

Overseas businesswomen are unlikely to encounter too many challenges in working in Hungary. During the communist period equality was, at least in theory, guaranteed within the constitution. After the transition, the level of employment among women decreased significantly as practical guarantees of equality were removed. Leadership positions in Hungarian business and government remain male dominated. Nevertheless, many women can be found at senior levels in all parts of the Hungarian economy, and are well-represented in the professions. In many organisations it is still common for men to flirt with women at work, including married women. Being professional and courteous and offering clarity around acceptable boundaries will normally be sufficient to enable business women to work as successfully in Hungary as elsewhere.

Be prepared to face questions about family, marital status and children. These can best be seen as sign of friendliness and a desire to place business visitors in a family and professional context. It makes sense to respond to personal questions in a positive way, giving as much information as you feel comfortable with.

Managing time, schedules, deadlines and bureaucracy

Corruption, minor and otherwise, was rampant in soviet-era Hungary and has remained a problem since then. For example, the Hungarian public health service tolerates the practice of patients paying doctors and nurses what is called 'gratitude money' for care which in theory they are entitled to receive free of charge. Gratitude money is institutionalised to the extent that both patients and medical staff see it as a normal part of attending a public hospital. A 2008 opinion poll suggested almost 40 percent of Hungarians viewed the payment of bribes to police officers, customs officers or tax officials as normal (although not desirable). There are continuing government attempts to deal aggressively with the problem of corruption, but foreign business visitors may well be faced with the problem of being asked to pay bribes.

Holiday seasons in Hungary are in July and August and mid-December to mid-January and it can be difficult to arrange meetings in these periods. Offices are generally open from 8am to around 5pm, with mid-morning or mid-afternoon the best time for appointments.

Punctuality is important and arriving even a few minutes late for a business meeting will create a bad impression. Attitudes toward keeping deadlines do not always betray the same sense of urgency, and it may be necessary for Anglo-Saxon business people to be a little clearer than normal as to the potential consequences of missed deadlines.